10 gifts OF wisdom

10 Gifts of Wisdom

What Every Child Must Know Before They Leave Home

Sally Clarkson

an ITJ book

HOME FOR *Good* PRESS
words for the heart

10 Gifts of Wisdom

Published by ITJ Books:
Home for Good Press
PO Box 345
Monument, CO 80132
www.itakejoy.com

Interior design and cover by:
Jeff and Joy Miller, Five J's Design, Texas
fivejsdesign.com

Published in the United States of America

TABLE OF CONTENTS

Dedication

Thanks to my dear, wonderful four children, best friends, who taught me what it meant to have godly character. My stewardship of your life taught me more wisdom than I ever learned any other way.

Thanks for Sarah Clarkson and Rachael Stroud for your brilliant, insightful ideas and help in making this book come to completion. I could not have done it without you.

And to Clay who always keeps us together.

Love all of you lots!

Introduction

"We are what we repeatedly do. Excellence, then, is not an act but a habit."

~ Aristotle

"HOW DID YOU RAISE all of your children to be so self-composed and polite?" I hear this statement often and it is inevitably followed by, "It must just be a Clarkson trait. It must have just been natural!"

How far from the truth! Excellence of character comes only through rigorous training, instruction, and practice. Every parent wants their child to grow up into a vibrant, gracious, competent adult, yet few today have a vision for cultivating those traits in their children. Giving children moralistic rules and policing their behavior is not enough to captivate their imagination in such a way that they will want to be men and women of strong character. What they really need is vision.

I realized this as I worked to nurture my own children early on. When Clay and I provided them with a vision for becoming compelling leaders in their generation, when we trained them to become skillful, challenged them to graciousness, they responded. By combining a compelling vision of what they could be with day-to-day training and encouragement, we prepared them to become influential with the messages of Christ in their lifetime.

Excellence of character is something that captivated my attention many years ago when, as a young missionary, I was challenged to move into Communist Eastern Europe to draw people to Christ. I accepted the challenge, and part of the preparation was a great deal of training. One of the pictures or ideas presented to us in our ministry training has stayed with me for years and influenced my parenting, and this is the idea that we were to be ambassadors for Christ.

An ambassador is a diplomat of the highest rank chosen to represent his or her country in a foreign land. As such, ambassadors must represent the messages, values, and wishes of the country they represent. They must also maintain the highest character so that their position of influence will impact the people they serve in the most positive manner for the country they represent.

I caught a picture in my young life that as an ambassador for Jesus and His kingdom, I was to represent His love by being generously loving and kind. As He is righteous, I was to be righteous, and practice integrity in front of the people I was seeking to reach. Truly, as an ambassador, I was to reflect the best of the One I was representing. Consequently, when God blessed me with children, I already had in mind that I would prepare them to become the best representatives, the best *ambassadors* for Christ, wherever He led them.

Manners, loyal love, a trained mind, a sense of God's purpose, spiritual vitality, character, gratitude; all of these themes and more are present in this book. The following chapters sum up what Clay and I considered basic training for our children as they became worthy warriors and ambassadors for Christ. Each chapter in this book covers some aspect of our goal to equip our children to gather the tools they needed to be strong in spiritual battle, to love well, and to build the self-image that would carry them through times of doubt and challenge. We wanted them to be formed with the character and skills they needed in order to flourish as adults and vibrant souls even in a fallen world.

Many children today learn principles of morality, but they enter adulthood without the kind of intentional training that will help them to stand strong, to live well, and to be faithful. So I am sharing with you the basic blueprint of the vision that provided each of our children with a strong foundation. I want to share the training, the habits, and the rhythms that we formed along the way that have prepared our children to stand strong in the storms and the beauty of life.

Even as an athlete must exercise his muscles to develop physical strength, so we exercise our own character and training muscles with children so that they can develop character strength. It is not a perfect science and it does not happen all at once any more than working out once lasts you for a lifetime. Personality differences mean that we will be stronger at some things than at others. Yet, the practice of training in this way will indeed produce a lifetime of fruit in you and in the lives of your children.

I have excerpted articles, ideas, and writings from a variety of places to put this book together, so the format varies from chapter to chapter. I hope this will be a potluck feast of stories, thoughts, suggestions, and encouragement. But I also hope that these principles will prepare your own children to have confidence, a sense of calling, and wisdom to walk the roads God brings their way.

May all of our children be worthy ambassadors for Christ and His kingdom.

Sally Clarkson
September, 2013

Chapter 1: Faith

The Gift of Living Spiritually

"Therefore as you have received Christ Jesus the Lord, so walk in Him, having been firmly rooted and now being built up in Him and established in your faith, just as you were instructed, and overflowing with gratitude."

~ Colossians 2:6

"Mother is the name for God in the lips and hearts of little children."

~ William Makepeace Thackeray

ASK ANY OF MY CHILDREN about their enduring memories of childhood, and one of them is bound to mention family devotions. They still chuckle about the Alpha and Omega day, when I drew an overview of Scripture on a chalkboard and told my ten-, eight-, and six-year-old children that God was the beginning and end of all things and their lives were part of his story. "Will you live by faith?" I passionately asked, and was met by their wide-eyed nods. To this day, twenty years later, they remember that devotional morning. They remember the rhythm of faith and prayer that set our days as a family.

They also recall the way that faith became real when they saw God actually answer our prayers. One particular morning stands out in all of our memories. The first years of Whole Heart Ministries were years that required great faith from us. We moved to the middle of nowhere, Texas, lived with my mother-in-law, and began to outline and write the messages we wanted to give to parents. But it was all very much by faith, and there came a time early on when Clay and I realized that we would run out of money by the next month. I remember that morning clearly; the bright Texas day and my children laughing and fussing, squirming in their breakfast chairs. We didn't tell the kids everything, of course, but we wanted them to be part of this life of faith, to take part as a family in trusting God. So when we came to prayer at the end of our devotions, we told them simply that we needed to see God provide for our family. Would they pray that too?

Their little faces grew very solemn (though this did not in the least stop their squirming). They squeezed their eyes shut where they sat at the table and each of them prayed in their high voices that God would give us what we needed.

Clay went straight to his office after breakfast, and the kids and I finished the dishes and gathered everyone to start the day. But before we could begin, Clay was back with news of an amazing discovery. On picking up the morning mail, he found a magazine notice for a particular lawsuit. He quickly realized that he had an interest in the suit and, upon calling the firm, discovered that this was the last day to put in his claim. The amount paid would provide for our family for the next few months. When we told the kids, their eyes were wide with wonder at the fact that God had answered their prayers.

"Mom," said Sarah, "God really heard us, and it worked."

The most important gift you can give your child is to help them begin a walk of faith with the God of the universe. From the moment your children arrive in your home, you are teaching them how to see the world, what to consider important, what to seek, what to love. As a mother, you have the opportunity to form your home and family life in such a way that God's reality comes alive to your children each day.

We live in a busy, pragmatic society driven by performance and activity. In the realm of parenting, this is a particular influence as we moms feel the pressure to provide the best education, the best lessons, and the best meals. We want our kids to have character, we want them to clean their rooms, and we want them never to be lonely and to have all the music lessons and activities that they want. But the thing your child needs most in the world is a heart that knows the love of his or her Creator. The greatest gift you can give your kids, a gift they will carry with them into each relationship and situation of their lives, is a heart deeply centered on loving God and a life formed by the habits of faith.

This requires you, as a mom, to have what I call a kingdom-mindset, an awareness of your life, and your family, as part of the ongoing story of God's kingdom. "Seek first the kingdom of God," said Jesus (Matthew 6:33), and the first part of your calling as a mother is to introduce your children not just to the reality of God, but to the knowledge that each of us is called to love him, to know him, to seek him daily, and to form our lives according to his will. It is in your home and presence that your children will learn what it means to be a follower of Christ.

The spiritual life at home is a practice of living, a way of seeing, and a habit of prayer that sets God and his kingdom at the center of all you teach and do. Paul affirmed that "in Him [God] we live and move and have our being" (Acts 17:28, NIV). The life you create in your home can communicate this reality every day. But it is vital to remember that the spiritual life isn't a list of rules you and your children must keep, or a schedule you must follow.

The kingdom life at home is a life centered on a relationship with God, an awareness of his presence, and love in the smallest details of your family. This includes cultivating habits of faith, making time each day for a family devotion, teaching your children to pray, and helping them to memorize scripture. But it is also a way of life that is a celebration of who God is. This life includes watching for His beauty in the changing of the seasons, thanking him together for life or health or unexpected grace, feasting on holy days, and cultivating a constant awareness of God's goodness at work in the world.

But you as a mom cannot give what you do not have. Before you can pass on a love of God to your children, you need to know that love yourself. You need to know Scripture before you can teach it to your children. Whatever it takes, you must plan for ways to nourish your own spirit, to keep your own heart close to God. For me, that meant getting up before my kids for a cup of coffee and some quiet time. It meant planning in specific hours when I could get away. It meant fellowship with like-hearted friends.

You must do whatever it takes to set aside a space of time each day to pray, to read Scripture, to journal. You need encouragement and accountability. Seek out friends and mentors who will keep you accountable in your walk with God. If like-minded souls are hard to find, start a Bible study or fellowship yourself. Read. Pray. Seek. The goal is to be sure that your own heart is rich so that when you teach your children you can give to them out of your own treasure.

One of the sweetest gifts of my life is to watch my grown children walk with God. When I have asked them why, despite the foibles or failures of our family, despite struggle and imperfect days (and imperfect parents), they caught the faith we were trying so hard to teach them, I find in their answers that it was the rhythms of life, the way of making God present that shaped them most.

"I love God because of bacon and French toast," said Sarah one day. "We ate and celebrated and enjoyed the goodness of the world. And as we did we talked about God, we prayed for what we needed, we admitted our struggles, we watched Him work. Faith wasn't just a subject on the side; it was our whole life."

The gift of a whole life of faith was exactly what I hoped to give my children. I don't think there's a greater one that I could give.

Family Rhythms of Faith

In the whole life of faith, one of the best ways to begin is simply to establish a rhythm of family habits that keep your home centered on God. The whole idea of these habits is that they are a regular heartbeat in the life of your home. The following habits are practices that will provide a framework of devotion, prayer, and spiritual cultivation to your days as a family.

Family Devotions

From the time the kids were little, Clay and I made sure that we read Scripture with them (however simple) and prayed every day. This never looked quite the same. Sometimes we were able to have that time as a family at breakfast, and Clay would work through a family devotional. Many times, he left early to work and I sat with the kids instead. We read *The Child's Story Bible* by Catherine Vos, or I read to them from my own Bible and we always ended in prayer. But our goal was to begin each day with Scripture, with a time in which we came together to learn about God and acknowledge Him as first in our lives. Here are some ways that might help you accomplish the same thing in your home:

- Set aside a time each day, whether at a meal, before bedtime, or early in the morning, when you as a family meet for devotions.
- Plan ahead and have a devotional or personal reflection to share with your kids.
- There are a variety of children's Bibles available and they are a wonderful way to expose children to the stories of Scripture. We loved *The Child's Story Bible* by Catherine Vos, as well as *The Jesus Storybook Bible*.
- Don't worry about perfection. Sometimes I did devotionals, sometimes Clay, sometimes we did them together. Each life and family will look different. Make your rhythms and your love of God unique to your own family's time and needs.

Family Prayer

Because Clay and I wanted our kids to understand themselves as part of God's kingdom, we made a habit of praying as a family. We taught the kids to come to God with needs, with prayers for missionaries or friends, with family concerns, or with special requests or praise. Prayer is one of the main ways we ushered our kids into the reality of God, letting them voice their own hearts to him, and then watching him work in their lives. And yes, your children will squirm and have a hard time keeping their eyes shut. Mine still do as adults. But fear not; the practice and the grace of those prayer times are deeply forming their hearts.

- Make a time each week when you gather specifically to pray as a family. Let each of the kids share their own needs or concerns. Let your children know some of your needs as a family, and let them enter into the faith you have that God will work to provide for you.

- Keep a prayer list. If you have missionaries you are supporting or sponsor children or friends with special needs, make a list and put it on your refrigerator. Then, whether at meals or special occasions, pray for those people and let your children pray for them specifically as well.
- Start the habit of bedtime prayer. Even my adult kids like to be prayed for before they go to bed. This can be a dear, comforting, and very memorable time for children in which you help them to remember God's love and comfort as they go to sleep.
- Remember to pray in times of crisis. When your children are struggling, when a friendship has been lost, or money is needed, remember to pray! Teach your children to turn to God in every situation, to bring their needs before Him.

A Personal Bible

When they are old enough to read and appreciate it, give each of your children a Bible of their own and help them to make time each day to read a little bit (even if it's mostly pictures) and pray. This sets a habit that will undergird their faith for the rest of their lives.

Joshua Stones

Every year, on a Saturday near Clay's and my wedding anniversary, our whole family celebrates what we call

"Family Day." We make cinnamon rolls and coffee and gather to read the passage from Joshua where the Israelites are instructed to create a memorial of stones so that they will remember the miraculous work of God. As a family, we write a list of all the ways God has been faithful to us. Jobs gotten, friends made, money provided, gifts received, dangers averted, we jot it all down (everyone gets to contribute as much as they want) and then we create some kind of memorial "stone." We actually used river rocks one year in Texas, but mostly each person gets a piece of paper on which to draw a memorial picture of the gifts or answered prayers that meant the most to them. Through the years, we have collected the lists and drawings into a red notebook that is a marvelous history of our family and a record of our faith in God as we saw Him work miracles in our lives.

Mom 'n Me Times

The best way for children to learn to love God is through the friendship and discipleship of their parents. In addition to family devotions, Clay and I made specific times each week in which we met individually with the kids. We listened to doubts or fears, we sought to know what was going on in their little hearts, we read hero tales together, or talked about what it meant to be a godly young man or woman.

- Create a time each week or two to meet one-on-one with each child. Make it a time of delight. If your daughter loves tea, make tea and scones just for the two of you. Or take a more active child on a walk in the park.

- Find a book or story that you can read aloud together that communicates some of the spiritual principles you want to teach. You could read a hero tale aloud, or a story from Scripture, or you could work through a devotional together and discuss the ideas each week.
- Make time to truly hear what is going on in the heart of your child. Let them know how special they are and how much you, and God, care for their individual needs, doubts, and hopes.

KEEP CALM AND CARRY ON MOM TIP

"Train up a child in the way he should go, even when he is old he will not depart from it" (Proverbs 22:6). Old is the emphasis here. The spiritual training you give your children forms them little by little, year by year. Don't despair if it takes time. Keep the larger vision in view.

WRAPPING UP THE GIFT:
PUTTING THE GIFT OF FAITH INTO MY CHILD'S LIFE

_____

_____

_____

_____

_____

_____

_____

_____

_____

_____

_____

_____

_____

_____

_____

_____

_____

_____

_____

_____

_____

_____

Chapter 2: Friendship

The Gift of Faithful Fellowship

"Iron sharpens iron. So one man sharpens another."
~ Proverbs 27:17

"Friendship is the greatest of worldly goods. Certainly to me it is the chief happiness of life. If I had to give a piece of advice to a young man about a place to live, I think I should say, 'Sacrifice almost everything to live where you can be near your friends.' I know I am very fortunate in that respect."
~ C.S. Lewis

As the sun set, casting shadows around our kitchen as I made dinner, my little girl walked slowly in and sat at the kitchen counter. Tears welled up in her round, brown eyes as she put her elbows on the counter and held her face in her hands.

"Mama," she started, and it all came tumbling out, "I thought that Christians were supposed to be different than non-Christians. I can't believe my friend would lie to me and then get mad at me for talking to her about it. It just doesn't seem fair!"

The whole story eventually came out through stops and starts of tears and sniffles. The cause of Joy's woe was a very close friend who had gotten angry, yelled harsh words, and stomped out when Joy tried to talk to her about a sensitive issue. I came around the counter and held my heartbroken daughter closely, helping her to wipe her eyes.

"How about we have a cup of tea together and talk about it?" I asked.

With candles lit a few minutes later, hot chocolate chip cookies ready to be dunked in milk, and tea steeping, I sat down with my sweet girl as she settled in on the couch.

"Mama," she started, "you always said, 'a friend loves at all times.' I didn't really know what that meant until tonight. Gossip and fighting and drama are awful and I don't really feel like loving. But that verse means I'm supposed to be committed to my friend, no matter what, right? Just like Jesus is committed to us, even when we sin against Him."

I nodded and squeezed her hand as her tears flowed again. She smiled a wobbly smile and leaned close to me.

"It really costs a lot to be a good friend, doesn't it, Mom?"

Friendship is an extraordinary and often costly gift from God, a beautiful reminder that we are not expected to do life alone. When we teach our children the value of true fellowship, encourage them in creating community, and help them to know how hard it will be, we are giving them the gift of learning to love well. We are instilling the skill of faithful, forgiving, cultivating love that will equip them to flourish on the unique journey that God has for them. Through the many joys, struggles, successes, and major disappointments that life may bring, it is a great gift to have community around us. But it is a gift that must be chosen, nourished, and sometimes renewed. Dietrich Bonhoeffer described the concept of Christian community eloquently in his book *Life Together.* He says this:

> "Christian community is like the Christian's sanctification. It is a gift of God which we cannot claim. Only God knows the real state of our fellowship, of our sanctification. What may appear weak and trifling to us may be great and glorious to God. Just as the Christian should not be constantly feeling his spiritual pulse, so, too, the Christian community has not been given to us by God for us to be constantly taking its temperature. The more thankfully we daily receive what is given to us, the more surely and steadily will fellowship increase and grow from day to day as God pleases."

As mothers, we have the powerful opportunity to teach our children the great value and worth of friendships. The way we model, encourage, and create fellowship is crucial to the way our children will learn to relate in their own adult lives. I never wanted my children to see themselves as loners, as people not responsible to love and bless others. I wanted them to perceive themselves as givers, as hosts, as true friends.

We were made to know God's love through the love we give and receive. We were made for close family friendships, for community, for relationships that last throughout our lives. But friendship is something we must fight to create. The hectic nature of modern life, the increasing isolation caused by technology, and just the inherent risk of dealing with sinful human nature causes many people to draw back into isolation. If you can teach your children to reach out, to be the ones who make connections, who truly see other people and voice their love and care, you will have equipped your children both to receive and give love in a powerful way. They will offer love to a world that desperately needs it.

But raising children who value friendship in this world is no easy task. Friendship has to do with the major heart issues we have to face in ourselves and in our children: knowing how to love, to forgive, to nourish relationships, to put others first, to be kind, to be patient. The hardest part comes as we teach our children to put others first. Thinking of ourselves and doing what we feel best satisfies us is natural—putting others before us, being humble, thankful, and selfless, is *supernatural.*

"Greater love has no one than this, that one lay down his life for his friends." (John 15:13)

I had my children memorize that verse. I knew that ideas like that, memorized and remembered, could call out truth to my children throughout the day. Mothers may sometimes feel overwhelmed and exhausted with these minuscule, routine, daily words of wisdom that we must speak over the lives of our children. However, my ministry began as a mother, simply taking the time to have patience and offer one word, one prayer, and one instruction at a time to the little ones who so desperately needed my direction. That's how hearts are formed, minute-by-minute and word-by-word.

The friendship you have with your children is the first example of friendship they will encounter. They need this friendship as a foundation and model for the other friendships in their lives. Nurturing times of fellowship with my kids was just as important as training their manners or confronting their behavior. Before my children could be good friends, they needed me, their mom (and dad), to befriend them.

They needed me to help them learn how to navigate the waters of friendship. I taught them how to be initiators. I invited them into special times with me and then helped them to invite and plan special times with their friends. I taught them how to prepare for their friends, to make cookies, light candles, plan activities, so that their friends would feel welcomed and loved. In my own relationship with them I taught them forgiveness, forbearance, and a self-controlled tongue. When they came home frustrated and angry at the offense of a friend, I walked them through the process of accepting and forgiving that person. Much of my authority came from the history of the friendship I had with my child, a history filled with the very forgiveness and acceptance I was asking them to have.

Throughout their childhood, I also kept in mind that the way I related to my friends would shape their view of friendship. I think that when we as moms view our relationships with others as a rare and beautiful gem, a gift to be treasured, we will be able to model what it looks like to nurture those friendships with a grateful heart. We will be teaching our children to honor and value others, to rise above selfishness, and to cultivate kindred spirit fellowship.

After all those years of teaching my children to invite people over, to have patience, to write thank you notes, to speak with grace, to be loving even when they didn't feel like it, I am now able to watch each of them flourish in their personal and professional friendships. They have learned how to appreciate and enjoy others. They know how to plan for times of fellowship. They know how to reach out and communicate love. That is a gift that will go with them wherever they wander.

Cultivating a Heart for Community

Teaching Your Children to Put Others First

"Humility is not thinking less of yourself, it is thinking of yourself less."

~CS Lewis

As a mother, you are faced with the challenge of a world that generally teaches people to think mostly of themselves. Your task is to help your children develop a Christ-like mind, heart, and soul in the midst of a culture that focuses on selfishness, instant gratification, and self-serving motives. Putting others first should be second nature to our children, but that will only occur if we are helping them to see the *good* that comes from selflessness. Instructing our children in the ways of what it truly means to put others before ourselves and to consider the needs of those around them will enable them to *be* great friends and *have* great friends. How does this happen?

Set a Good Example

Little eyes will always be watching to see what we are modeling for them. Are we displaying an example of people who serve joyfully? Or do we dread putting others first and see it as a *daunting* task? In your own friendships, model the same behavior that you would hope to see in the children you are raising. As your little ones watch your interactions, they will learn and be inspired by your own selflessness.

Opened Eyes

Teach your children to open their eyes to the needs of others. Talk to them about various situations that others are in, and how they would want to be treated if they were in their shoes. Focus on the Golden Rule: "So in everything, do to others what you would have them do to you, for this sums up the Law and the Prophets" (Matthew 7:12, NIV).

Opened Ears

Being a good listener is a crucial aspect of becoming a great friend. Encourage your children to be slow to speak and eager to listen. Role-play with your little ones and do a mock "interview." A great way to make friends is to show interest in others by being someone who asks *questions*. Practicing within the family is a wonderful start, and will be most comfortable prior to taking these skills and using them on new friends. Teach your children to show interest in others, and start with your own family. Let your children interview you about your own story, or ask each other about their day. Make the dinner table a place and time of discovery, with each person finding out new things about the others. When we ask questions, we are showing others that we care about what they have to say.

KEEP CALM AND CARRY ON MOM TIP

Unfortunately, no miraculous, "perfect behavior" pill has been invented yet (as each of us could probably use it at one point or another). Raising selfless children is a lifelong process. Some days will be better than others, just as they are for us. Remember to have patience and give your children grace when they struggle and fight the very natural, human desire to be selfish. Never forget that we also have our days when we have fallen short. Love your children with your whole heart, even on the difficult days.

Sharing is Caring

"*Mine*" is one of the most common early words to be uttered from a toddler's mouth. From a very early age, our sweet little ones learn that something can *belong* to them, and shortly after comes the desire to become very possessive and controlling about almost *everything* in sight. Selfishness in toddlers, and the desire to "own" everything, is an early attempt to set apart and create their own unique identity in the family. This is a very natural, normal process, but it's not so fun when bad attitudes, screaming, and tantrums come into the mix. It's also a habit that needs training in the right direction so that a child learns to consider himself a giver, not a taker. Sharing is about seeing the needs of others, learning that enjoying something *with* a friend is better than keeping it all alone. Cultivate sharing in these ways:

- Encourage sharing by purchasing books and toys that do not exclusively belong to just one child. Of course, there are special things that each child will hold as their own. But if a general attitude of community is nurtured, children will learn to hold toys, books, and possessions with open hands instead of grasping ones.
- Encourage them to give a toy, a note, or a hug as a gift to a sibling. Help them to take what is theirs and share it with another. Consider having a once a year "clean out the toy box day" when children can choose which of their toys they want to share with someone else, perhaps donating to the less fortunate.
- When your children get to the age where they are going to a friend's house to play, it is crucial that you as a mother clearly express what their level of expectation should be. Talk to your children about being respectful of others' belongings, and remind them that it is a privilege if their friend decides to share a toy or item, but it isn't something that they are required to do. Remind your children to be good friends, good sports, and good at sharing even if their friends are not doing the same.

KEEP CALM AND CARRY ON MOM TIP

Practice makes perfect. As children start playing with others and learning to cooperate, they will begin to see the value of sharing.

Create Community

One of the first things that friendship requires is for someone to initiate. "Hey, do you want to come over for tea?" Those words can be the first in a long story of a deep and lifelong friendship. But that will only happen if you train your children to be those who initiate, who invite, who prepare for the people they love, and create a space where fellowship can happen.

Saturday Pizza Nights

Invite another family over once a week for an evening of talk, good food, and games. Let your children prepare in choosing a fun dessert, setting out cups and plates, lighting candles, and creating a welcoming environment for your friends.

Small Group/Class/Discussion/Book Club

Start a small group study with several other moms who have kids about your age. Include your children in the study with you. You could create an "Inklings Fellowship" like my Joy did, and discuss the works of C.S. Lewis and Tolkien, or you could start a Bible study for teen girls, or a character and camping club for boys. Foster community by bringing it into your home and let your kids help with every aspect.

Friend Dates

Your daughter has probably watched you have friends over for tea since she was little. Or your son has noticed his dad meeting a friend for study. Let your children plan a special date with a friend and prepare for it with your help.

Thank You Notes

Raising my children to be people who write thank you notes has made a significant difference in the course of their lives and friendships. Writing thank you notes can be what sets your child apart from the rest of the crowd after an interview for colleges, career, and more. But it is also a way of connecting with the people you love, affirming how and why you are grateful for them, and touching base to keep a relationship vibrant and alive. Thank you notes teach articulation of relationship. While our generation may view cultivating handwritten notes to be "old-fashioned," it is a special way to show respect, honor, and love to others. Here are some tips to get you going:

When is the right time to write a thank you note? Anytime! There is really never an occasion in which writing a thank you note wouldn't be appropriate. Thank you notes should be written:

- After someone has given you a gift of any kind.
- If someone has had you over for a special dinner or event.
- When someone has done a special favor for you.
- After an important interview.

Is my child too young to write a thank you note? Your child is never too young to participate in the thank -you note process. From the time my children were just learning to write (and could just barely write their own names), I would talk to them about what they were thankful for or what gift was extra special to them. Next, I would write the thank you notes for their birthday gifts and other occasions and simply have them write their names at the bottom. They would be in charge of decorating the note, drawing pictures, and making the note "pretty." This is a wonderful way for your children to start early on the route to gratefulness.

What should I include in my thank you note?

- Clean, neat handwriting.
- A greeting with correct spelling of the name of the person you are writing.
- As basic as it may sound, you should always express what you are *thankful* for in the note. If it was a gift, write specifically what the gift was and why it is so special to you. Consider including a photo of you using your gift. (If they got you a gift card, tell or show them the goodie you decided on ... a picture of you wearing the backpack grandma and grandpa got you ... etc.)
- Affirm what you love about the gift *and* the sender. Articulate what they mean to you.
- You can end a personal thank you note with warm regards (*love, best wishes, yours truly, etc.*) and end by signing your name.

KEEP CALM AND CARRY ON MOM TIP

The more your children practice writing thank you notes, the more confident they will become. This can be a fun, creative task and a wonderful learning experience. Take the time out of your day to sit down with your children and practice writing thank you notes as a family.

WRAPPING UP THE GIFT:
PUTTING THE GIFT OF FRIENDSHIP INTO MY CHILD'S LIFE

_____

_____

_____

_____

_____

_____

_____

_____

_____

_____

_____

_____

_____

_____

_____

_____

_____

_____

_____

_____

_____

_____

CHAPTER 3: CHARACTER

The Gift of Loving Virtue

"The good man brings out of his good treasure what is good…"

~ MATTHEW 12:35

"I hope I shall possess firmness and virtue enough to maintain what I consider the most enviable of all titles, the character of an honest man."

~ GEORGE WASHINGTON

"**Y**ou never let me get away with a single thing, Mom!" My sixteen-year-old daughter faced me with a dramatically tragic face and tears in her big, blue eyes. "Why can't you just understand that I'm a teenager? All of my friends have attitudes too and their moms let it slide. I'm just feeling emotional." Her eyes were snapping now.

I sighed. Confrontation, especially of my children, is about my least favorite thing in the world. All I had asked was that Sarah empty the dishwasher and load the dishes. The roll of her eyes, the mutterings under her breath ("It's *always* me; the boys *never* help") and the thump of her reluctant feet had prompted me to suggest that perhaps work was simply part of life and that she had a choice to make about her attitude.

Our confrontation at the sink, as with most confrontations, continued far beyond that dishwashing moment. We talked afterward. I showed her Scripture. I reminded her of our standards as a family. I hugged her. I encouraged her. I sent her upstairs to recover and to have some time to think and pray. And then I sat back on the couch, exhausted, knowing very well that ten such conversations might happen again the next day with four of my sweet and sinful children in the house.

Moments like that contained some of the most important work I did as a mom. I knew then and I know even better now that my children's lives would be irrevocably formed, their hearts trained, their characters shaped by just those confrontations. When my babies were born, I had grand visions for them. They might be missionaries to Africa, or great writers (like Dickens or C.S. Lewis), doctors who cured cancer, or musicians (Bach, Beethoven?) who changed the world. But as I was confronted with four little ones with self-centered hearts and strong wills, I quickly realized that one of the hardest, but best roles I would ever play as a mom would be a trainer of character.

"He who is faithful in small things will be faithful also in much."

I think that sentence is burned into the brains of my children. It was one of my mantras as they were growing up. Now that they are adults, they smile as they recount how often I repeated that phrase to them. But I repeated it because I was convinced that if my children didn't know how to be faithful in the smallest details of life—housework, sibling relationships, parental honor—God would never be able to trust them with the great deeds that needed to be done in His kingdom. And since I had decided from the beginning that I was raising kingdom-hearted heroes, I trained away.

As I did, and as I turned to Scripture for encouragement, I quickly realized that what I was doing as a mom was just what Jesus did with his disciples. Day after day he taught, modeled, and trained them in what it meant to love and honor God. He was there to answer every question, to confront every wrong attitude, to shape every conversation. He lived day in and day out with twelve men who would eventually change the world. One of my glories as a mother has been the realization that I have the chance to form the hearts and life habits of my children. Clay and I together had the never-to-be-repeated opportunity to train them to godliness from their earliest years.

One of the first ways we did this was to list out the character standards for our family and home. We came up with twenty-four "family ways," each backed with Scripture, that we decided would define our home life, work, and relationships (Clay later turned this into a devotional resource for families). They included such expectations as:

We love others with kindness, gentleness, and respect.
We serve humbly through thinking of others first.
We are thankful whether we have a little or a lot.
We make peace even when we feel like arguing.

We listed them out and went through them with the kids during our devotions. We had the kids memorize the Scriptures that supported each family way. We discussed our family standards regularly, and referred to them as part of confronting sinful attitudes. By creating a family culture based on biblical virtues, we gave our kids an atmosphere in which character training was simply part of everyday life, a normal expectation for our family.

It was certainly one of the greatest challenges I faced as a mother in that it was an every day activity. More like every hour. Habit training is one of the hardest things you will ever attempt. An excellent character is the result of countless conversations, habits, confrontations, and daily interactions. The process was constant, as I helped my kids to take part in housework, settled fusses, modeled (and enforced) gracious speech, or insisted on the completion of a task or faithfulness to finish a book. This was why having the family ways and the Scripture behind them was so important. I had a standard to which I always returned. I wasn't making things up on the spur of the moment, or asking arbitrary things of my kids. We all knew the standard by which we wanted to live.

Another great challenge we faced was simply the cultural climate. The art of character, the idea of a person formed by the classic virtues such as humility, diligence, and honor is one that I sometimes miss in modern culture. I often feel that we live in a world where nothing is sacred, where everything can be a joke, and where sarcasm is the rule of most conversations (especially those you see on TV). As I looked around me at the way culture was going when my children were young, I turned to the stories of historical heroes to help them understand what virtue looked like.

We read all sorts of books about historical and biblical heroes. The kids pored over the *Childhood of Famous Americans* series and loved the *Your Story Hour* dramas of the lives of virtuous men and women like Booker T. Washington, Abraham Lincoln, Eleanor Roosevelt, Louis Pasteur, and David Livingstone. We read dramatizations of biblical stories and plied our kids with the virtue and beauty of classic children's literature. We knew that part of character training is the formation of a moral imagination, an inner idea of what it looks like to be virtuous. We wanted our kids to have plenty of role models to follow.

I am tickled now whenever I hear my children repeat the old family ways or tell someone "He who is faithful in small things will be faithful also in much." I've launched four kids into adulthood and it is one of my greatest glories to see them practice diligence in their work, to watch them relate with honor and grace to difficult people, or ask each other for forgiveness when they are wrong. They're far from perfect. Spend one night with all of us in the house and you'll know that for sure. But they *are* men and women of excellent character. I have watched them respond, grow, and strive to become even better than they are. And I know that all the daily, difficult, never-ending training was worth it.

"You never let me get away with a thing," Sarah said that again to me the other day. But this time, her eyes were wide with something almost like wonder, and her face was gentle with gratitude. "All those times when you could have saved yourself so much stress by just ignoring my attitudes, you confronted me. You trained me. Mom, you've saved me *years* of misery!"

I smiled. I was just so glad she finally understood.

Creating Character

Create Your Own Ways

As a family, decide what your "code of conduct" will be. Base it on Scripture, and make a list of family standards that define the attitudes and behaviors you will practice in your home. Clay wrote *Our 24 Family Ways* when our children were young. We memorized the different ways with the kids and used those "ways" and the Scriptures we put with them to hold our kids to a certain standard of godliness in speech, action, and behavior. When they transgressed one of our ways, we always returned to it, explained its importance, and used the associated Scripture as a way of helping them to understand what was right or wrong in their actions and attitudes.

You may find inspiration in reading some older books on the subject of character and virtue. Though titles such as *Beautiful Girlhood* (originally published in 1922) or *Tiger and Tom* may seem old-fashioned, they present an ideal of character formation that you can adapt to our own culture and to your own family. The Victorians especially placed a high value on duty and honor, and there are some wonderful old books that can be very inspiring in the realm of character development.

Confront Sin

Confronting my children's sin is one of my least favorite things to do. I love harmony and I love to be close to them. But I knew that if I let their complaining or ungraciousness or whining go unchecked, I would be training them to weakness.

When your children struggle with a certain attitude, talk with them first. Explain why their response is wrong and how God wants them to respond instead. Point them to Scripture. Have them memorize a verse that is pertinent to their situation. Set consequences. Make it clear that they have a choice to make. Don't become weary; keep training, keep on loving, and keep confronting

Housework – the Daily Character Boot Camp!

I've included another whole chapter on housework in this book, but I will emphasize it again here. The ever-present reality of keeping house with a family presented us with a natural training ground for our children. From the time they were little we assigned chores and trained them (slowly but surely) to diligence. This is where the most basic character habits are formed.

Community/Church Service

Having the accountability and encouragement of friends and mentors can be a huge incentive to help children learn to become excellent. We had our kids involved in helping out with a Sunday school class, putting shoeboxes of gifts together at Christmas time, helping out at a homeless shelter, or simply cleaning the house of a neighbor or friend. The accountability of having other adults encouraging them to work hard and to serve well helped our children to see themselves as members of and contributors to the wider community. Character training is, in many ways, about giving your child an identity as a trustworthy person. Community can contribute to this in a powerful and positive way.

KEEP CALM AND CARRY ON MOM TIP

Inspiration and vision are key words in the development of character. Amidst the training you do on a daily basis with your children, make sure you are continuously articulating your vision of what you hope they will become.

Character Studies

Have your children pick a favorite historical character and do a study on the habits, attitudes, and actions that made their chosen person great. When he was nine years old, Nathan did a character study of Audie Murphy, a WWII hero, and then gave a presentation to a group of friends on Murphy's courage in battle, his initiative and ingenuity when faced with problems, his perseverance when all hope seemed lost, and his good attitude throughout. Nathan beamed as he gave that speech, and I knew at the end of it that he had a new idea of excellence for himself. Gather biographies, movies, and books and help your child to get well acquainted with the habits of heroes.

WRAPPING UP THE GIFT:
PUTTING THE GIFT OF CHARACTER INTO MY CHILD'S LIFE

_____

_____

_____

_____

_____

_____

_____

_____

_____

_____

_____

_____

_____

_____

_____

_____

_____

_____

_____

_____

_____

_____

_____

WRAPPING UP THE GIFT:
PUTTING THE GIFT OF CHARACTER INTO MY CHILD'S LIFE

_____

_____

_____

_____

_____

_____

_____

_____

_____

_____

_____

_____

_____

_____

_____

_____

_____

_____

_____

_____

_____

_____

CHAPTER 4: MANNERS

The Gift of a Gracious Presence

"Let your speech always be with grace, as though seasoned with salt, so that you will know how to respond to each person."

~ COLOSSIANS 4:6

"Life is short, but there is always time enough for courtesy."

~ RALPH WALDO EMERSON

I often wondered if my children were listening to everything I taught them. Their progress in life and godliness sometimes felt painfully slow, especially when it came to manners. Nathan, my very extroverted child, was a particular challenge. He disliked rules and was prone to say whatever came to his mind. No matter how hard I sought to give him a sense of honor for others and a grid of graciousness through which to relate to all people, I wondered if any of my instruction was really taking root.

One summer, Nate was invited to spend several weeks by himself at a friend's home. He was deeply excited, as this presented an adventure all his own and would also be the first time he had taken a plane by himself. With a dozen motherly admonitions, I sent him off and told him to be sure to call me when he arrived safely. My phone rang that evening and as I answered, his excited voice bubbled over through the receiver.

"Hey, Mama, it was so much fun to fly by myself. And you will never believe what happened! The stewardess talked to me off and on the whole flight because I had a seat at the front. I remembered to ask her questions instead of doing all the talking. I thanked her when she served me. I told her I appreciated her kindness to help me when I was looking for my seat. She said, 'You know, Nathan, you are one of the most polite boys I have met in a long time. It was really a pleasure having you on my plane!' Can you believe she said that about me, Mom? I felt just like I was an adult!"

When I had recovered from my shock, I smiled and congratulated him as heartily as I could. In the midst of that proud mama moment, I realized that all of those minutes, hours, days, weeks, and years of hard work and training had truly paid off. After all of those times when I wondered if Nathan was listening, I realized that he had taken it in after all. He actually knew how to be polite! Renewed in my resolve, I kept on with my training. And Nathan got even more when he got home.

Manners are essential to anyone who wants to lead or succeed in the world. A person who can speak with confidence, greet new acquaintances with poise, converse with grace, and even eat well at a social dinner has a set of skills that will enable them to be a presence of grace in any setting in the world. They will be able to "be all things to all people" as Paul said in 1 Corinthians, or as Kipling would have it in his poem If, "to walk with crowds and keep their virtue, or talk with kings, nor lose the common touch."

But it is vital to perceive manners not as old-fashioned rules, or a set of silly social behaviors, but rather as a way of extending grace to every person you meet. At heart, social and spiritual poise is about becoming skilled in relating to other people, setting them at their ease, and maintaining a sense of self-control in every new situation. Manners communicate grace.

When you teach your child to sit up straight, keep their mouth closed and use a napkin instead of their sleeve, you are giving them the ability to influence others simply because they know how to behave. When you show your child how to shake someone's hand, look them in the eye and greet them with respect, you are instructing your children in the art of respect, in showing honor to adults and new acquaintances. When you teach them poise, how to stand still without fidgeting or how to handle awkward people, you are giving them an inner strength that will serve them in every new job, home, or country they enter.

Many mothers despair of teaching their children manners, and we do live in an increasingly casual culture. Children don't take to manners naturally, as Nathan (and all of my children) so often proved. But while this may not be an area of spiritual import, I do believe that training our children to have good manners will shape the kind of people they become and the kind of lives they live. Just as ambassadors are trained to be able to relate and reconcile disagreements in different countries, manners equip your children to enter a myriad of situations that they might not otherwise be able to. Training in manners can be an important aspect of preparing our children to go wherever God calls them.

"Train up a child in the way he should go, even when he is old he will not depart from it" (Proverbs 22:6). As with all training, the formation of manners is a daily work. Every new acquaintance, every mealtime, every interaction with an adult is an occasion on which you can train your children's manners. At first, you may wonder if any of it is taking hold at all. But keep on, saying the same things again and again ("Don't talk with food in your mouth!" or "Hold the door open for your sister!"). Prepare your children before social events or before guests come over, asking how they will greet them, or what kind questions they will ask.

But remember in the midst of the training to talk to your children about what it means to be stewards of God's love. When we know God and call ourselves His followers, we are showing the world what God is like with every word and action. Manners are just one more way of communicating His kindness. Manners communicate respect, they confer dignity, and they offer grace. In the words of Elsa Maxwell, "Etiquette—a fancy word for simple kindness." A person with manners is using them in the best possible way when they understand that they are a vessel through which God moves in showing love to others.

Manner-Making

The Basics

There are countless books on etiquette available today, and when I was training my children, I looked through quite a few in order to gain a vision for the manners I wanted to instill in my children. In the end, I came up with a basic list of manners and social skills I wanted my children to have, and it became my guide as I trained. Though you will no doubt add a few of your own, here is my list if you need somewhere to begin:

- *Table manners.* Among other things, my children needed to know the proper use of silverware, how to put their napkin in their lap, chew with mouth closed, keep elbows off the table, and how to wait for the hostess to take the first bite.
- *Meet and greet.* First impressions are more powerful than we like to admit. I was adamant that my children know how to give a firm handshake, look an adult or new acquaintance in the eye, and introduce themselves with poise. It was also

important that they know how to address their elders with respect.

- *The art of conversation.* This is simpler than it sounds and involves mostly the skill of asking questions and giving thoughtful answers. I wanted my children to know that they were responsible to talk to other people, to create conversation in situations, and to communicate interest in the people around them. This also includes knowing that it is wrong to interrupt someone else (especially an adult).
- *Being a host/ess.* The demeanor and welcome of a hostess can change the whole way someone feels upon arriving in her home. I wanted my children to learn how to welcome with grace, how to greet confidently, how to show guests where to go, and how to take care of their coats.
- *Poise.* In every situation, regardless of their impatience or irritation, I wanted my children to learn the hard skill of poise. This simply meant self-control of emotion and body language in public places. It meant being able to overcome fear in order to give a short speech or meet a new person. It meant learning to control frustration and not vent anger in public.
- *Honor.* One of the major skills I wanted my children to learn in the realm of manners was honor for adults and a respectful attitude toward authority. All of my children are generally strong-willed, so I knew it was important to cultivate an attitude of humility in them and to help them understand that honoring elders is part of honoring God.

Practice Makes Perfect

One of the most beneficial aspects of learning to have excellent social skills is that they enable you to feel confident in any situation. Encourage your children and provide an outlet for them to practice these skills by creating circumstances in which they will be able to step out and test the waters.

Ladies Lunch

It is never too early to take your children out for some quality time to learn basic skills that will stick with them forever. Take your daughter(s) out for a ladies lunch. Have them dress up and get into whatever fun, dainty outfit they choose. Encourage your girls to look at the menu and order for themselves. When your little girls are responsible for ordering their own meal, they will practice speaking to an adult and engaging in conversation. While you are at the table, teach your ladies some basic etiquette such as putting their napkin in their lap, praying before the meal, chewing with mouth closed, not talking while chewing, and keeping their voice down while in a public place. This doesn't have to be an expensive or extravagant event. My little ladies have very fond memories of practicing these skills even over affordable sandwiches and tasty French fries. (You or your husband can instill the same skills by taking your sons out for a boys' brunch.)

Ring, Ring!

Phone calls are an excellent way for your children to practice speaking to adults and grow in confidence. Talk to your children in advance about what kinds of questions they should ask the person on the other line (How are you?

How is your day going? What have you been doing lately?). Practice in advance by doing role-play with your children. Stand back to back, and pretend that you are "Grandma" and have your child rehearse engaging in confident, polite conversation.

Talking to Adults

The entire time I was raising my four children, our home was often filled with guests. This was a wonderful opportunity for them to get constant, first-hand learning experience in conversing with adults. Carrying on conversations with grown-ups can be extremely intimidating, especially for children who are naturally more shy and introverted. Encourage your children to speak with the adults in your home; don't just let your children disappear to their rooms. The more practice your children get, the better.

Asking Questions

Teach your children to be people who ask questions. Asking questions and being a great listener is a truly important social skill. You will capture the attention and hearts of those around you when you are genuine, authentic, and care to hear how someone else's day is going. Inquiring about someone else not only shows your interest in them, but it is a wonderful way to keep the conversation flowing and put an end to any gaps of silence in the midst of your chatting. Practice this with your children on a regular basis, and prepare them before any family outing by asking what questions they will put to their friends or new acquaintance.

Policy of Politeness

Practice the policy of being polite with your children by going over your family ways. Talk to them about topics of conversation that are appropriate while greeting guests (asking questions, complimenting them, talking about the weather, telling them about a new skill you've been working on, etc.) and topics that your house guests probably don't need to know about (letting your children know that it's okay not to share their story about how nauseous they were when they had the flu last month)

Role-Play

Practice different potential situations with your children. Role-play and allow them to practice how they would talk to an adult so that they feel comfortable and confident in those circumstances rather than quietly hiding behind you.

KEEP CALM AND CARRY ON MOM TIP

If your child is practicing talking on the phone with Grandma and there is a gap filled with silence, smile and encourage your child. Give them the "thumbs up" to boost their confidence and remind them that they are doing a great job simply by trying. You can even make little cue cards with the reminders of what questions they should ask. That way, if your child forgets what they were supposed to be chatting about, they won't be filled with fear, embarrassment, or a sense of failure. These cue cards are a huge help for the quiet, introverted child.

The Importance of Body Language

Statistics have proven that 93% of all daily communication is nonverbal, making body language the most prevalent way that we interact with one another. Talking to your children about body language will help them immensely in many aspects of life. Regardless of intention, body language can make us look rude, disinterested, or bored if we aren't careful. But mindful body language can communicate that we are interested, engaged, polite, and respectful. Be clear about this in advance. Don't get angry with your children when they are yawning and crossing their arms at a party unless you have clearly explained this aspect of social skill and helped them to use it.

Monkey See, Monkey Do

Practice standing in different positions and modeling different habits, and clearly explain to your children why this is so important. Show them how to walk straight, how to shake a hand, and how to greet an elder. Have your child tell you a story, or something that happened in their day that is really important to them. While they are speaking, tap your foot, wiggle around, yawn, and cross your arms. Then, tell your child to start over. This time, look at your child, engage in the conversation, nod your head in agreement, and smile. Talk to your child about how they felt the first time versus the second attempt.

Eye Contact

Encourage your children to look others in the eyes while they are speaking. This is not only polite, but it also lets the speaker know that you are truly interested in what they have to say. Many shy, introverted children struggle with looking people in the eye due to a lack of confidence. Studies have shown that darting of the eyes, looking away, or closing the eyes is a subconscious blocking behavior. This occurs when we feel intimidated, worried, anxious, or bored. Use the steps listed above in the "encouraging confidence in every situation" section to help boost the self-esteem of your child so that they feel equipped to look people in the eye and engage in conversation.

Fidgeting

Moving around and fidgeting is our body's natural way of dealing with stress, insecurity, and anxiety. Help your children learn to breathe deeply, to be aware of their movement, and to fix their attention on the person before them. Talk to your children about what certain body movements might communicate to the person they are with. Shoulder shrugs make us look bored and disinterested. Fidgeting, tapping feet, and looking away communicates nervousness and a desire to be away.

WRAPPING UP THE GIFT:
PUTTING THE GIFT OF MANNERS INTO MY CHILD'S LIFE

_____

_____

_____

_____

_____

_____

_____

_____

_____

_____

_____

_____

_____

_____

_____

_____

_____

_____

_____

_____

WRAPPING UP THE GIFT:
PUTTING THE GIFT OF MANNERS INTO MY CHILD'S LIFE

_____

_____

_____

_____

_____

_____

_____

_____

_____

_____

_____

_____

_____

_____

_____

_____

_____

_____

_____

_____

_____

_____

Chatper 5: Service

The Gift of Giving Yourself

"For even the Son of Man did not come to be served, but to serve, and to give His life a ransom for many."

~ Mark 10:45

"Make it a rule, and pray to God to help you to keep it, never, if possible, to lie down at night without being able to say: "I have made one human being at least a little wiser, or a little happier, or at least a little better this day."

~ Charles Kingsley

I was in quite a hurry on the rainy day we pulled up to a stoplight in Nashville and saw a weather-beaten man on the curb holding up a dripping sign. I had both of my boys with me, they were seven and five, and we were late to their weekly music lessons. Windshield wipers thumping, streetlights gleaming through the rain, I glanced at the bedraggled figure standing outside our car, but I couldn't stop today. There simply wasn't time.

"Mama," Nathan's voice piped up from the backseat, "look at that man in the rain. Look, he has a sign. He must be cold."

"'Homeless: anything helps, God bless.'" Joel read the words off the damp sign. "Look, Mom, he only has one leg."

For a moment, Joel contemplated this with a solemn, sad little face, and then he turned to me, eyes big and urgent.

"Mom, we should help him. We should buy him a hamburger!" I glanced at my watch and scouted the busy street for fast food restaurants. There were none in sight. But Joel, seeing the hesitation in my face, leaned forward from the back, straining against his seatbelt. "Come on, Mom," he urged, "he really needs our help and you said we should always help the people God puts in our way."

So I did. Clay and I were always telling our kids to keep their eyes open for the people God might put in their lives who needed their help or kindness. We wanted our kids to see themselves as servants, to have an identity as givers. I couldn't contradict Joel's impulse to give. I decided that music lessons would simply have to wait and I rolled down the window.

"Hello, sir," I said as the man moved stiffly toward us, "my boys want to buy you some lunch."

"Ask him if he wants hamburger or chicken," called Joel, while Nathan added his own high-pitched command to be sure of his favorite drink. The man told me what he liked and we took off as the light turned. By the time we found a McDonald's, ordered the perfect meal (with many directions from my boys – "Supersize it, Mom, he looks really hungry!"), and made it back around to the stoplight, the rain had lifted a little and the man shuffled over to meet us.

As I handed him the bag of hot food and the supersized soft drink, the boys piped up from the back with, "We got you a hamburger like you said, and lots of French fries!" The man took the food, then put his hands on the window and leaned into the car.

"Boys," he said looking back at each of them, "thank you so much. You're the first people who stopped all day. What are your names?" the boys told him, and the man nodded, "Well, thank you Joel, thank you Nathan. God bless you."

"What's your name?" piped up Nathan from the back as the man turned to go.

"Michael," he said simply, and with a nod to me, walked away.

That night, as I put Nathan to bed and prepared to pray for him, he looked up at me with a very serious face. "Let's pray for Michael, Mama," he said, and that began a month in which the boys prayed fervently for Michael, "their homeless man," every night. As I watched their little hearts ache for the loneliness and hurt of another person, I thanked God that I had taken the time to stop, to live out the message I was trying so hard to teach them every day in our home: how to have the heart of a giver, the heart of a servant.

From the time our kids were old enough to listen, Clay and I told them over and over, "I wonder how God will use you in the world. I wonder whose heart you will heal or what truth you will bring." We wanted our children to think of themselves, even when they were little, as someone who had a responsibility to give, love, and to serve the people around them.

One of the main goals of our training was for our children to leave our home with a sense of personal mission, the conviction that they were called to be the hands and feet of Christ in the world. Clay and I both came to marriage with a background in ministry, so this was part of our identity and vision for our family to begin with. But the model that drove our training of our children didn't come simply from our backgrounds, but from our study of Christ and His kingdom. Our ultimate goal was to raise children who walked closely with God, who knew His love, and who brought His kingdom to bear on earth. The cultivation of a servant's heart in our children was simply one of the most vital ways to connect them to the reality of the gospel, to help them understand their lives as part of God's story.

One of the common criticisms of children raised by careful, Christian parents is that they think the world is all about them. Their parents spend so much time investing what is good in their kids and giving them everything they need that they make them self-centered. The kids then have the expectation that the world owes them something, instead of understanding their lives as a gift, and the love they have received as a treasure that they must give out again. Then, too, we live in a "me" culture, an age of consumption and distraction that wants to convince children and young adults that the goal of life is to get, not to give.

To teach servant-heartedness is a radical departure from the way of the world because it is to teach your children the way of Christ, who gave up his whole life so that we could know his love and grace. Training your children to have a servant's heart isn't about completing a list of service projects or giving a certain amount of money. It is about giving your children the core identity and self-image of a giver. They need to know that they are called to follow in the footsteps of the God whose kingdom story they are called to live.

As I worked to create this identity in my children, I learned that there is a process by which such a self-image is formed. The first part had to do directly with me as a mother. Before my children could embrace servanthood, they needed to see their mama do it first. I quickly learned that my attitudes about work, my moods as I cleaned or cooked, my joy (or lack of it) when company came were immediately communicated to my children. Their attitudes were a mirror of mine. If I complained, they complained. The best way I could teach my children to serve with a joyous heart was simply to do it myself.

But I also found that when I took the time to serve them personally, their hearts softened and they were willing to listen to my training. Joy, my youngest child, has always responded to gifts of service. I am not a detail-oriented person, so I don't always think of these things, but one year, when we were going to be out of town a lot, I had the idea of helping Joy pack her suitcase, something she usually did on her own. She had seemed particularly moody and unhelpful in the past few days. But I sat on the floor in her room, helped her select outfits and shoes and fit them all into her suitcase. The longer we sat, the chattier she got, and I watched her countenance soften. When I stood up at the end, she hugged me and said, "Thanks for serving me, Mama. I know you're busy, but it means a lot to me."

Your children will never know what it means to serve in love, to truly offer their time, their homes, and their resources to others unless they experience it first in their own home, and from their own parents.

The second part of the process was having my children serve with me. Clay and I involved the kids in almost every aspect of our ministry from the start. Sarah and Joel sealed envelopes and stamped newsletters, all of them babysat kids of the parents we counseled, they served at conferences, and carried suitcases for the moms who came to our ministry events. "If it is God's will for us to be in ministry, it's God's will for you to be too," we said. We started every conference with an evening of training for our kids and the volunteers, talking about why we ministered and what kind of heart we wanted to have.

When we traveled, the kids often had to sleep on the floor or watch the children of host families as ministry events were going on. At home, several of my mom friends and I arranged for our kids to sing and perform a short drama for the residents of a nearby nursing home. My boys worked several days each Christmas with a shoebox ministry. By involving our children in every aspect of ministry and seeking out opportunities for them to serve at home, we hoped to pass on our own vision of our family and ourselves as servants in God's kingdom.

But we also cultivated a culture of servanthood at home. It's far easier to serve a stranger than a sibling. We worked hard to create a culture of kindness in our home. When one sibling was having a hard day, we encouraged the others to make them a cup of tea, take over a chore, or even just give them a few kind words. We trained them to speak graciously and to serve one another by refraining from criticism or harshness. Day by day, word by word, we trained our kids to be givers, not only to the world, but also to each other.

The third part of the process was equipping our children to give and serve in their own unique way. This was an exciting process as we sat down with each of them once they were old enough and asked them what God had put on their heart to do for other people. Their answers were as diverse as their personalities. Sarah wrote letters to several lonely elderly women. Joel gave all of the coins he had saved for a year to a homeless shelter. Nathan did magic tricks for a group of little kids. Joy volunteered to mentor young girls. We helped them to gather whatever they needed, we encouraged, we prayed, and then we let them give. I will never forget the glow on Joel's face when he gave his money to the shelter.

"Mom," he said, "I think it really helped them."

So it did. But it also helped him to see himself as a giver, and that is a gift I hope he carries with him all his days.

Practicing Servanthood

Different Kinds of Service

Servanthood doesn't come in the form of work alone. God calls us to serve with our hands, yes, but also by speaking truth, by comforting, by giving, by loving, even by creating something new within the world. Consider how your own family, with your unique set of gifts, could serve in any of the following ways. Be creative, have fun. Some of our best memories as a family center around the times we served together.

Practical Work

What are some hands-on jobs that you could do to serve a neighbor? What needs doing at your local church? Weed a garden, vacuum classrooms, clean a friend's house, cook a friend a meal (and let the kids help!).

Messages

Sarah is my introverted girl, but I knew she had a lot of wisdom and love she could share with young girls. I challenged her to put together a talk and begin a small Bible study. She was a little overwhelmed at first, but when she shared what she had learned in her quiet time and watched the girls respond, she glowed. "I think God really used me to tell them something," she beamed.

What messages do your children have within them? What truth do they know? What truth needs to be spoken into our culture today? Help your kids identify the ideas they are passionate about and find a place to speak or write them to an audience.

Who could your children mentor? Once you know truth, you become a steward of it. One of my best friends says all discipleship should be up and down; in other words, you should have someone above you as a mentor, and below you as a disciple. Are there friends or even siblings that your own children could teach? Challenge them to serve by their influence and words.

Hospitality

The art of hospitality is one that will serve your children throughout their lives. It's also one of the most enjoyable ways to serve as a family. Make a practice of hospitality in your home by inviting another family over at least once a week. Let your children be part of all the preparations, cleaning, cooking, decorating, lighting candles, and arranging flowers. Teach them to understand that the preparation of the house and the giving of the meal is a way of showing love to those invited.

Role Models

Do a specific study of biblical heroes who were servants in the Bible. Let each of your children pick someone specific, such as David, who tended his father's sheep, or Ruth, who worked in the fields, or Jesus, who washed His disciples' feet. Have them do a character study, listing out how each hero served and what they communicated by their love.

Mentors & Friends

Find a way to serve with others in your local community. The joy that comes when many people work together is something that could deeply impact your children and will help them to feel part of a fellowship in which everyone serves.

- Get several families together and let the kids learn several songs or put together a short drama, then perform it at a local retirement or nursing home. My children did this with friends for many years and still love to remember the way the residents smiled, sang along, and sometimes even cried.
- Round up a gang of your older kids and challenge them to take on somebody's yard work for a day. Make a great picnic and praise them to the skies and tell them to see how much work they can get done in one morning.
- Seek out mentors who will allow your children to minister with them. One of my dear friends gives health and nutrition classes and lets teenage girls assist her with the kitchen work. Another friend works with foster kids and trains teenagers how to be mentors to kids from broken homes.
- Have a "pounding" for new neighbors or just-moved friends. This is an old term for stocking a new kitchen with a "pound" of all the necessaries.

Sponsorship

There are numerous wonderful aid programs through which you can sponsor a child overseas. Choose one together as a family, and have regular times of prayer for the child you support. Challenge your children to earn money to contribute toward what the family gives or to write letters to your sponsor child.

KEEP CALM AND CARRY ON MOM TIP

Cultivating a heart of service in your children can be lots of fun. One season of particular loneliness for our family found us all a little blue. As we were pondering what to do, one child excitedly suggested, "Let's make dozens of cookies and surprise every friend we love and take all afternoon to deliver cookies and tell everyone how we appreciate them!" Soon all our "woe is me" attitudes were turned into "giving is fun!" attitudes. It was such a delight to get everyone involved. Even little three-year-old Joy caught the spirit and helped. It took us all day, but we took cookies to everyone. And as a result, many of our friends ended up asking us over for lunch, meeting us at the park, and telling us how very much our love gift meant to them. To this day, my children bake something, make "I love you" flower bouquets, or create a special card to give to those they love as a surprise.

WRAPPING UP THE GIFT:
PUTTING THE GIFT OF SERVICE INTO MY CHILD'S LIFE

_____

_____

_____

_____

_____

_____

_____

_____

_____

_____

_____

_____

_____

_____

_____

_____

_____

_____

_____

_____

_____

WRAPPING UP THE GIFT:
PUTTING THE GIFT OF SERVICE INTO MY CHILD'S LIFE

_____

_____

_____

_____

_____

_____

_____

_____

_____

_____

_____

_____

_____

_____

_____

_____

_____

_____

_____

_____

_____

_____

CHAPTER 6: WORK

The Gift of Purposeful Industry

"Make it your ambition to lead a quiet life and attend to your own business and work with your hands."
~ 1 THESSALONIANS 4:11-12

"Teaching children the joy of honest labor is one of the greatest of all gifts you can bestow upon them."
~ L. TOM PERRY

In the early years of our ministry when we were just getting everything off the ground, there were months when our whole family would be out of town for four or five days at a time. Clay would then have to leave for another several days after that. Managing my four children, cooking, teaching, and giving Joy her middle of the night asthma treatments had left me raggedly exhausted. One day, in the midst of this tumult, Sarah (13) came into the den as I was straightening up from a very busy day.

"Mama," she said, "we kids have a favor to ask you. Would you mind going to the store to get some ice cream so we can have a fun night together? We have a little surprise for you!"

Unable to bear the thought of disappointing my bright-eyed, expectant children, I wearily climbed in the car, bought ice cream and a few other groceries and got home thirty minutes later. By the time I reached the door, weariness was a weight on my shoulders. I stumbled in.

I looked up and immediately realized that the place was transformed. Candles were lit. The den was straightened to perfection. As I walked through the house I saw that dishes and pans had been washed and put away. The two baskets of laundry from my bedroom were folded and distributed. My sheets were turned down with a little note from all of the kids, (even a few scratchy letters from three-year-old Joy). The heartwarming note read:

Dear Mama,
We know you are tired without having Daddy home. But
we wanted you to know how much we loved you and
appreciated you. Let's have a fun night and you can even go
to sleep early and we will put ourselves to bed!

Love,
Your Children

Sarah, of course, as the oldest child, was the instigator. But all of the kids had pitched in to give this gift to their mama. They had all grown up helping me daily with the chores. They knew how much work a family like ours required, and how much it would mean to me that they had taken the initiative to complete it on their own. Their surprise was an even greater gift to me than they knew because it showed me that they were beginning to see themselves as capable workers in our home.

From the beginning, I knew that the gift of a good work ethic was one of the vital things I wanted to pass on to my children. I knew that their attitudes toward work would greatly influence their vocation in life, their relationships with authorities, and even the harmony of their own future homes and families. Work is a central part of life, and I knew that my children needed to embrace it if they were going to flourish as adults.

The word "work" often comes with negative thoughts and connotations. We tend to see any kind of labor as a necessary evil, something we have to get out of the way before we can relax. But work is something created even before the fall. God meant us to work, to create, and to beautify the realms with which we were entrusted. Work is part of what we were created to do in the image of God. In our role as mothers it is crucial that we model and teach a healthy work ethic to our children.

The very definition of a work ethic can be summed up as the principle that hard work is intrinsically good, virtuous, or worthy of reward. In a generation of constant stimulation, television, children with iPads, couches, and potato chips, instilling good work ethic into the lives of little ones is no easy task. Because we live in a fallen world, work is hard, something children aren't born necessarily to love. We all have days when we just want to give up. But each and every day, I had to make the choice to continue encouraging my children, modeling great habits, and working hard to help them develop a sense of purpose in the work they did as members of our family.

As mothers, we know that it is important to instruct our children in the basic habits that will help them to flourish in every aspect of their lives. Each of us hopes we can watch our children succeed in every avenue they pursue. A good work ethic is foundational to this hope. When children learn to work with diligence and excellence, they have a firm base under their feet. Without this foundation, it is difficult to form any healthy or long-lasting habit, but with it, any dream or goal may be attempted.

Delving into Scripture is always a wonderful way to begin helping your children to understand what we are accountable for and expected to subdue. Start with the first few chapters of Genesis. Read God's blessing over Adam and Eve and his commission to them in Genesis 1:28: "Be fruitful and multiply, and fill the earth, and subdue it; and rule over the fish of the sea and over the birds of the sky and over every living thing that moves on the earth." From the first of creation, we were meant to work, to subdue the earth and make it beautiful. Far from originating as a punishment, work was the place we were to find our greatest fulfillment.

Even after the fall, when work became hard, God still affirms the goodness of work. God never encourages laziness, but expresses very clearly that each of us should work together and do our part. Psalm 128:2 says: "You will eat the fruit of your labor; blessings and prosperity will be yours."

I love this verse because it presents the simple truth that labor is worthwhile, beautiful, and valuable. Words like work and labor can make us feel exhausted and defeated before we even begin the task. But that Psalm points to the fruit of what labor brings. We work for a purpose. Ecclesiastes 5:12 tells us that "the sleep of the working man is pleasant." It is our job as mothers to point out the beautiful blessings and benefits that come from working hard and helping out.

I believe in rewarding children for a job well done. Our kids earned little treats or prizes for excellent work when they were young. When they were older, their diligence and faithfulness earned more freedom and our trust in their judgment as we gave them time with friends or trusted them with an independent project. God meant work to bring us fulfillment and, while not all tasks come with a prize, it's a delight to set your children's work ethic by rewarding their efforts when they are young.

But an excellent work ethic is also about identity. Before we can expect our children to help out and work hard, we as moms must first examine the way we think about work. Ask yourself: do you take pride in your work? Do you work with a joyful heart? Do you view your work as a blessing? These are all very important questions to consider because your answers might shed some light onto how your children view things like chores, helping, cooking, and other tasks in the home. God has entrusted you to steward an incredibly important job. Mothers are called to subdue and bring life, joy, and beauty to each and every aspect of what it takes to care for the sacred place we call home.

Remember that God has made you the model for your children. No matter what you are doing or what attitude you choose to maintain, little eyes will always be watching, and their ears are constantly listening to how their mama handles the tiny tasks that each new day brings. If you dread cleaning the dishes and complain about it each and every night, your children will automatically develop that same sense of hatred for the dishes before even accomplishing the chore. If your heart is full of resentment each time something needs to be done, your little ones probably won't feel any different about the job. When your children see your attitude of pride and joy in caring for your home and conquering new skills, it will inspire them to do the same. Your goal is to make them independent workers. Cultivate a self-image that says, "This is my room and my house. I need to take responsibility to keep it clean."

The cultivation of a work ethic is a daily work in and of itself. When you have your attitude and vision in the right place, all that remains is faithful training. Repeatedly reminding my children to pick up their socks, wash the dishes without complaint, keep their rooms lovely, and complete their tasks thoroughly may not have been my favorite part of mothering. But it was one of the most vital. Those tiny habits, those daily chores, helped to shape my children into adults who could work long, hard, and well in every aspect of their lives. Their ability to work frees them to attempt anything they can imagine.

Working Toward a Great Work Ethic

Start with Chores

The work of the home is a basic training ground in work ethic for your children. This ever-present, daily work provides a natural arena in which you can help your children to practice diligence. Don't do everything for them. Instead, involve them in the upkeep of the house and the preparation of meals from the time they are small. Not only does it train their habits, it makes for great friendship as well. Before you even begin, though, keep in mind a few basic ideas to provide a framework or plan as you assign different tasks to your kids.

Chore Charts

Make a basic list of responsibilities for each of your kids. Put it on the refrigerator, or somewhere visible so that they can see what is expected of them each day. Setting expectations is crucial to a good work ethic; if children don't know what is required of them, then they have no goal to work toward and you have no basis on which to require their cooperation.

Incentive

There is nothing wrong with rewarding your children to help them learn to work well. Give small treats or prizes when a child makes his or her bed for two weeks in a row. Create a point system by which your children earn points for each task successfully accomplished, and set different point levels of rewards from little (stickers, a piece of candy) to big (a date with mom or dad, a movie night out).

Encouragement and Expectations

Have a family meeting every so often to help your children know what you expect and require of them. Encourage them when they are working well and recognize their achievement. Help them not to feel that what you require is random, but that there is a system of which they are a part.

Chores for Little Children

Even at a very early age, you can begin incorporating a helpful, servant mindset in your little ones. Finding age appropriate chores will boost your children's confidence and help them to feel that they are a necessary part of a family that works together as a team. These are also the basic daily habits of cleanliness that your children will carry with them into adulthood.

Dirty Dishes

After meals, encourage your little ones to bring their own plates to the sink. If they are a bit older, they can even go ahead and rinse their dishes and place them into the dishwasher. Even older? Even better! Have your children be responsible for fully washing their own dishes completely after dinner. And, of course, teamwork makes the dream work: encourage your children to take turns washing dishes for each other. This will help them develop a heart for serving others.

Make the Beds

Making one's bed is a habit that needs to be taught early on, but once instilled will last forever. From the time they are tiny, train your little ones to pull their sheets and covers straight when they get out of bed each morning.

To Each His Own Room

Help your children to value a lovely bedroom. Encourage them to straighten their toys each morning. Put baskets in their rooms to be a keeping-place for toys, crayons, stuffed animals, and other odd things.

Musical Sweeping

Mothers have the ability to make cleaning look like fun! Turn on music from Mary Poppins and give your children brooms. Encourage them to dance like Dick Van Dyke in the chimney sweep song. An ordinary day of chores can be transformed into a musical extravaganza!

Life is Crumbly Sometimes

Dust busters are a great age appropriate way for children to help around the house. Next time there is a crumb, allow your child to man the dust buster. This is not only a helpful and necessary task, but kids find it extremely fun as well.

Oops, I Spilled

Raising children who wipe their own spills is a lifesaver for moms and also develops great skills in their own lives. Fight the urge to control, stress, and immediately clean. Have patience and allow your little ones to wipe up their own mess. Simply hand them a paper towel the next time there is a spill.

Which One of these Doesn't Belong?

Sock matching is a fun, challenging game for children, a puzzle that desperately needs to be solved. Place your laundry on the carpet or bed and ask your little one to help you match all the socks. This is a very exciting challenge for little ones, and it really makes them think. It can also be educational as they focus on matching, paying attention to patterns, textures, shapes, and colors.

KEEP CALM AND CARRY ON MOM TIP

Don't worry, there are lots of ways to inspire young workers. Create a colorful chore chart. Have your children choose the color of poster board, and allow them to decorate it with stickers and various colors so that it is beautiful and exciting for them.

Chores for Older Children

When you have put in the time and training to raise little ones with helpful hearts, they will become a great blessing to you when they are older. As my kids grew in age, I began to trust them with more responsibility, allowing them to own or oversee certain tasks. They also became involved in the deeper cleaning of our home and knew that they each had a certain job to fulfill.

Once-a-Week Deep Clean

I always took one morning a week to clean the house at a deeper level. As soon as they were old enough, I showed the children how to clean bathrooms, vacuum, wash windows, and other tasks that would help us care for our home as a team. Sarah liked being in charge of wiping all glass surfaces. Joel preferred the vacuum, and he was also my occasional expert polisher of silver. The older they got, the more discipline and initiative I required of my children in their work. I wanted them to do it because *they* were excellent, not just because I told them to.

Morning and Afternoon Straightening

Twice a day, I had my kids help me in a basic straightening of the house. To Josh Groban music or the challenge of a timer, we'd rush through, picking up toys, washing dishes, straightening pillows, and making everything lovely, either to start the day or to welcome Dad home. Daily straightening was the expectation of our family and something I had the older kids take full responsibility for once they were able.

Getting Outside

Doing yard work is a great way for your older children to help out while getting some fresh air and sunshine. In the fall, raking leaves stretches them to a capacity of hard work that will give them stronger muscles to accomplish more. Shoveling snow, mowing the grass, and helping with a garden accomplish the same.

Setting a Beautiful Table

When your children are older, you can give them free reign in setting the dinner table in a way that is beautiful and pleasing to them. This is a wonderful task for those who are creative, as they can use their eye for design in choosing dishes and silverware, candles, or a centerpiece. Allow them to decorate the table however they see fit, creating a seasonal arrangement or lighting lots of candles.

Committing to a Specific Skill

Work isn't just about cleaning. As your children grow older, one of the arenas in which they must learn to work hard is toward their vocation. Help your children to choose a specific skill and then be faithful to work at it long term. Music lessons provide a wonderful opportunity. Physical sports are a possibility, or artistic endeavor. The learning of a musical instrument or the training of the body requires hard work, dedication, and commitment. These are skills that are crucial to living as an adult, and when your children reach their goals within this kind of endeavor, they will discover a healthy pride in their work that will equip them for further goals. Remember that every child is unique. Talk to your children about what they love. Help them to master a skill that delights them.

KEEP CALM AND CARRY ON MOM TIP

Try this A.B.C.D.E. acronym if you need a jolt of inspiration.

A Affirm your children when they are attempting a new task. If your youngest child picked up a crumb off of the kitchen floor, tell them how much you appreciate their help.

B Boost them up and cheer them on! You are their cheerleader. No matter how tiny the chore may be, always say, "Great job!"

C Confidence is key. The entire point of instilling work ethic into the lives of your children is so that they can feel confident and capable of taking on responsibility.

D Dedicate time to training them. Set aside specific quality time for work so that you will have the margin and patience you need as they try and fail.

E Encourage your little ones, even when they fail. Don't get frustrated if your seven-year-old doesn't clean the windows exactly as you would. Praise them for the work they can do.

WRAPPING UP THE GIFT:
PUTTING THE GIFT OF WORK INTO MY CHILD'S LIFE

_____

_____

_____

_____

_____

_____

_____

_____

_____

_____

_____

_____

_____

_____

_____

_____

_____

_____

_____

_____

_____

_____

CHAPTER 7: GRATITUDE

The Gift of Generous Thanks

"In everything, give thanks; for this is God's will for you in Christ Jesus."

~ 1 THESSALONIANS 5:18

"Piglet noticed that even though he had a Very Small Heart, it could hold a rather large amount of Gratitude."

~ A.A. MILNE, IN WINNIE-THE-POOH.

On a blustery fall day, I stood in the kitchen with my thirteen-year-old Nathan. Out the window, the crimson oak leaves swayed in the wind and the first autumn storm threatened rain. Inside, all was coziness and candlelight as the kids got the living room ready for a morning of read-aloud. Nathan and I had been assigned to make coffee for the group and, as we waited for the water to boil, we stood at the window.

"Look at the colors, Mom," he said, nose pressed against the glass. "It's amazing out there."

I nodded as the kettle shrilled and Nate turned to help me select the mugs, heap coffee in the filters, and pour the boiling water through. As I spooned sugar and cream into the other cups, Nate took his aside, and with the air of a master chef began to make his perfect cup of coffee. After the prerequisite sugar and cream, he went in search of whipped cream, piled it to the top, then pulled the cocoa powder from the cabinet and sprinkled just a dusting over the top.

"Look mom," he grinned, "it's a masterpiece."

Taking a sip, and licking away the whipped cream, he rolled his eyes at the deliciousness of it all. Holding the mug out to for a toast, he spread his arms wide.

"God is absolutely the best, Mom! He made coffee, and cream, and chocolate and," pointing to the window, "fall leaves and storms and everything! He didn't have to make us with taste buds, but he did, and life is amazing!"

I smiled. "Nate," I said, "you are absolutely right. I hope you always remember that."

Children are born with a natural capacity to wonder. They arrive in the world shaped by God to touch and taste, to explore, to see. They are like sponges, soaking up the beauty of the world as they encounter it through their senses, and they are quick to marvel at the richness of the creation around them. One of the best gifts that you can give your child is to help them to preserve that childhood habit of wonder, to continue, even into adulthood, the habit of receiving the goodness of the world as a gift. In other words, you can teach them to live by a habit of gratitude.

What does it mean to live a life that is shaped by constant thanks? "In everything give thanks." It is one of those Bible verses we hear but do not necessarily heed because it seems impossible. Right before it comes "rejoice always and pray without ceasing," verses using absolute words of command. Always. Everything. Why is the giving thanks so central to the Christian life, and why is it truly one of the most vital habits you can give to your child?

Because at heart, gratitude is a constant remembrance of God; His presence with us, His goodness, His beauty as it plays through creation. Gratitude is a way of life, and it is the daily choice to perceive every good thing that comes as a gift from the Creator. It is also the choice to meet the dark and broken things that come with faith that the Creator will make them new. By teaching your children to live with this view of the world, you are equipping them to meet life with curiosity, to meet struggle with courage, and to have a foundation of joy that will see them through times of celebration and of grief.

But as with every aspect of child training, it is a rhythm of life that has to be kept every day within your home. The training is often joyous affirmation, as it was for me with Nathan in the kitchen that day. You can cultivate wonder in your children simply by taking them outdoors on a nature walk, telling them to find the treasures that God has made and hidden in the world. You can nourish gratitude by the words you speak, articulating wonder in every aspect of life, from the variety of spices and foods to the changing of the seasons.

You can deeply cultivate gratitude by helping your children to recognize God's blessing within your family's life. Let your children know when God has helped you through a hard situation financially, and let them witness his provision. Help them to see gifts of friendship, or the grace of a new community, or the provision of a new opportunity as a gift from his hand. To give thanks in everything means cultivating a view of the world in which God's goodness is never absent, but is the cause of every good thing.

But there is also a more difficult side to the cultivation of gratitude, and that is the work of combatting the attitudes of discontent, boredom, and envy. Because we live as fallen people in a fallen world, the wonder that is the gift of childhood is quickly submerged in discontent as children are exposed to the larger world. In our stuff-saturated, instant gratification, fast-food culture, we are driven to consume, to buy what makes us happy, and to buy it now. Children are quick to pick up on this culture. When the kids were small, we noticed that whenever we took them to Wal-Mart to shop with us and they encountered the overabundance of the toy section, they inevitably grew whiny afterward, wanting this toy or that thing, unhappy when we refused.

Many parents today feel that if they do not provide their children with every possible toy, experience, entertainment, lesson, or thing, they are failing their kids. But happiness doesn't come with an abundance of things, and godliness certainly doesn't. Joy comes from a heart shaped by the habit of thanks, a heart that takes pleasure in every aspect of life. We were diligent to train those attitudes of discontent away, to talk them through with our kids, to help them see entertainment and things not as a right, but as gifts for special occasions. And when those gifts came, they were bright, special moments for our kids.

Sarah distinctly remembers the elation she felt at a picnic when a friend of mine handed her a *whole can* of root beer. Used to splitting things with her brothers, she turned to me with wide eyes and asked, "Do I get to drink the whole thing by myself?" She still recalls the pleasure of that drink and told me recently of a conversation she had with a friend.

"Mom," she said, "we both decided that we were really thankful to have grown up in our parents' lean years, when we couldn't afford everything. It taught us to enjoy life, to really see every gift, every meal out or trip as something special."

A grateful heart is a humble heart, one that does not demand but receives, and gives again, with joy.

Gratitude also taught my kids, and me as I worked to model it to them, how to meet suffering. Though gratitude seems on first glance to be about all the good things of the world, it is intricately connected with how we greet what is hard, broken, and bad. The natural human response to suffering is despair, and there is nothing wrong with sorrow. But as we move through the sorrow, we have the choice to respond to suffering with faith, to look beyond our grief to the God whose love promises to heal and redeem all that is broken. In my life, I have found that one of the most powerful ways of acting out this faith is through affirming

God's goodness right in the midst of struggle, and that is through celebration.

My kids told me recently how much they learned as they watched me handle one particularly hard evening in our family. There was a period of several months when Clay had to be gone five days a week and I was by myself with the kids. We were tight on money, in the midst of a church dispute, and I was struggling with health. One night, after a particularly hard day, Clay left for his workweek and I was left once more with the kids. As I shut the door, I knew that they were watching me, wondering if I would be sad for the rest of the evening.

I sighed, turned around and said, "Okay everyone, let's have a picnic on my bed and watch a movie tonight. Joel and I will get cheeseburgers. Sarah, you make cookies. Nate, you and Joy pick a movie." Their faces went from apprehension to excitement in an instant. They scurried to get everything done and ended with a small feast on my bed, cuddled next to me as we watched an old adventure movie. They told me recently that the way we celebrated that evening helped them to understand what it meant to create light in the midst of darkness, to choose joy, which is the practice of a grateful heart.

To be thankful at all times is to "walk in the Light, as He Himself [Jesus] is in the Light" (1 John 1:7a). To give thanks is to dwell in the joy of God. To live in wonder is to encounter beauty every day, and it is also a source of courage in facing the battles of this life. By giving your child the gift of a grateful heart, you are equipping them to meet every aspect of their life with a secret source of strength. To be thankful at all times is to dwell in the life of God.

Habits of Gratitude

Cultivating Wonder

One of the easiest ways to nurture a grateful heart in your kids is simply to give them the time and space to wonder. Be sure from time to time to turn off all the screens in your home, create time for creativity, and give your children the chance to explore. Here are some ways we did that with our own kids:

- *Draw.* Equip your kids with notebooks and pencils (and a snack to sweeten the deal) and send them outside. Tell them to collect five treasures and draw them in their notebooks, or write a poem about what they found.
- *Feast.* Let your children help you plan a feast of their favorite things. Involve them in the process of shopping for ingredients, making the food flavorful and colorful. Talk with them about the variety of tastes and scents in the world and make the whole process a celebration of God's bounty.
- *Stars.* On a warm night, take your kids out to watch the stars. Put a blanket on the lawn or deck, lay on your back, and simply enjoy the beauty.
- *Adventure.* Take your kids for a mountain drive (or ocean or forest or country drive) and picnic. Put on beautiful music and sing your lungs out. Call it a day of celebration and tell them to watch for all the ways that God created good things – food, music, family, earth, sunsets, wildflowers, etc.

Articulating Thanks

Words are powerful in shaping our lives. What we speak creates a narrative that reveals what we think about life. Help your children to articulate wonder, to practice the habit of speaking thanks.

- *Give thanks.* Make a family practice of identifying the good things that happen in your life. Whether at dinner time or at bedtime prayer, or simply in the car on the way home from an event, practice the habit of expressing thanks for friends, meals, beauty, experience. Create a culture of spoken gratitude in your home.
- *Thank you notes.* Teach your kids to write thank you notes. This is a basic of etiquette and training, a skill that will take them far in adulthood. But it is also a powerful way of helping them to express thanks, to recognize and honor the generosity they meet in others.
- *Counteract complaining.* When your child is whiny and discontent, ask them to name ten things that they are thankful for instead of complaining.
- *Bedtime.* As part of bedtime prayers, have your children thank God for the beauties, small or large, that they have encountered during the day. One of my friends keeps a yearly planner by her bed, and uses the spaces for each day to list what she was thankful for that day. You could keep a similar book for your children, a record of blessing they can look back on as a history of God's goodness in their lives.

> ## KEEP CALM AND CARRY ON MOM TIP
> *Gratitude is so much about the way we see the world. Cultivate wonder in your own heart and you will see it reflected in the hearts of your children. It's a simple habit.*

Special Celebrations

Of course, Thanksgiving Day is an excellent day on which to practice the art of gratitude, but there are other special days or traditions you can create to be times of thanksgiving for your family specifically. Here are some ideas we have enjoyed:

- *Five Kernels.* On Thanksgiving Day in my house when I was a child, everyone had to take five kernels of dried corn from a basket when the meal began. At the end, the basket was passed round again and everyone had to name five things they were thankful for as they put the kernels back in.

- *Family Day.* Create a Family Day just for your family. In our house, once a year, we put aside a Saturday to sit down with cinnamon rolls and coffee and list out all the ways that God has been faithful to our family. Jobs gotten, friends made, trips taken, help given, we list it all out and write it down so that we can be aware of the goodness of God ever-present in our lives. We have a family time of prayer and praise afterwards, our high day of giving thanks to God.

- *Once-a-week celebration.* Set one meal a week as a time of thanks – make it a feast, whether a Sunday dinner or a high tea, and let everyone share the highlights and joys of their week. End with prayer.

Recognizing Grace

Especially in our culture, it is easy for children to be unaware of how blessed they are. Once in awhile, gently expose your children to the harsher realities of children around the world and help them to be aware of all that they have.

- *Sponsor children.* If you sponsor a child overseas, find pictures and information on their living conditions. Compare a day in the life of that child to a day in the life of your kids.
- *Simple meal.* Have an occasional "Third World" dinner. Once in awhile, I would make a very simple dinner, something like plain rice or beans, and we would spread blankets on the living room floor as a family and eat our dinner by candlelight alone. This simplicity and lack of usual abundance helped to give our kids a taste of the simpler, starker realities in other parts of the world.

WRAPPING UP THE GIFT:
PUTTING THE GIFT OF GRATITUDE INTO MY CHILD'S LIFE

_____

_____

_____

_____

_____

_____

_____

_____

_____

_____

_____

_____

_____

_____

_____

_____

_____

_____

_____

CHAPTER 8: HOSPITALITY

The Gift of Living Graciously

"Do not neglect to show hospitality to strangers, for by this some have entertained angels without knowing it."
~ HEBREWS 13:2

"Hospitality isn't about inviting people into our perfect homes, it's about inviting them into our imperfect hearts."
~ EDIE WADSWORTH

Joy lit the last candle as Sarah scooped the last bit of raspberry soup into the old crystal bowls. After fifteen years of hosting a Christmas tea for all of our friends, each of us now specialized in a specific task. Joy bedecked the table with delicate crystal and hand-painted floral china inherited from a great grandmother. Sarah made the cold raspberry soup we had learned to love on a visit to Hungary, and also baked the cream scones that we served with clotted cream and strawberry jam. I whipped up the cold chicken salad with roasted pecans, red grapes, onions, a dash of curry, and mayonnaise and yogurt dressing. Chocolate mousse cake had become the traditional desert with Joy's whipped cream and chocolate sauce as the adornment.

Giving our friends an appreciation tea and luncheon, complete with a Christmas ornament, had become an event that grew in importance over the years. Each year, along with our old and dear friends, we also invited two or three girls that we thought were needy, lonely, and in want of special encouragement. This particular year, we invited a precious young woman who had grown up in such a broken home that she barely knew that kindness and thoughtfulness existed. Her rough background had hardened her heart toward people and given her a defensive posture toward the world.

The tea went as usual that year until the end. Each person was given a small gift of appreciation and the annual ornament as we told stories of how much each had meant to us. I noticed my special guest growing increasingly quiet, but she seemed happy amidst all the other women. After the meal, as many of us chattered in the kitchen at the end of the lunch, washing dishes, straightening the table, and enjoying the last few minutes of fellowship, the young woman sheepishly walked over to me and tapped me on the shoulder.

"May I speak to you, please?"

I nodded, and before she could even begin she began to cry. I took her into the other room and we sat down as she told me her story.

"I am thirty-five years old and I have never even had a cup of tea in a real cup. I had read stories in magazines of friendships like this, but until today, I didn't even think they were possible. I just want you to know you have given me the best Christmas gift I have ever had; a sense of *belonging*."

In all my years of ministry, I have found that very few people have a sanctuary, a place of refuge where they know that they are loved and accepted. Home is an illusive dream for many, something they hunger for but never expect to find. As I created a rich home for my own children, weaving an atmosphere of love, of beauty, and of shelter, I realized that it was also a gift to share. As we invited people into the natural rhythms of our family, or had them to dinner, they were able to taste a sense of belonging that they had rarely known. As I included our children in this increasing ministry, I quickly realized that the gift of hospitality was one of the practices I most desired to pass on to my children.

Home can be one of the most deeply transformative places in the world, a refuge where hearts are shaped and God is known. As a mother, you have the power to create a small, life-giving world within your home. The rooms of your home reflect your values, your tastes, but, most importantly, your love. Home should be a beautiful land where people are loved, where God is known in the meals and memories made, and belonging is offered to all who enter.

God has entrusted mothers to be the makers of homes, the cultivators of beauty, and the lovers of life. This has been one of my greatest delights as a mother. However, He didn't mean us to create this abundant life and then keep it all to ourselves. When you practice hospitality, you are inviting the lost and lonely into the refuge of your family and the love you share. Imagine God placing the key to your home directly into your hands. He is doing so to bless you and your family, and also so that your family may open the doors to your home and invite others in.

The amount of people who have told me that they never get invited into a home shocks me. What has happened to the art of hospitality? God is the great host, inviting all of us into his kingdom, to share in his feast and live in his beautiful city for eternity. We are called to imitate him in all that we do, and hospitality is a powerful way of reaching hearts. With a simple invitation, you can open up a new world of love to someone who has never known family. With a feast or a cup of tea, you can extend the love of Christ to a lost heart. And you can do all of this in your home with your children, teaching them to love and serve right alongside you.

It all begins with the delightful art of hospitality. Some of my most precious memories with my children come from the times that we prepared our home for others. In opening our lives to be a place of encouragement and shelter for other people, we recognized the great gift we had in each other. I have watched each of my children move into their own adult spheres and immediately carry on the hospitality they learned as children. They have learned the secret of love that is the foundation of a great home: love exists to be shared.

Honing the Skills of Hospitality

Gain a Vision

If you are new to the idea of your home as a place of refuge for others, begin with Scripture. If you can catch the vision of what it means to create a home and invite others into you love, you can pass that on to your children. Look at these verses:

In his letter to Titus, Paul says, "Rather, he [an overseer] must be *hospitable*, one who loves what is good, who is self-controlled, upright, holy and disciplined" (1:8, NIV). Hospitality is one of the qualifications for someone who wants to lead within the church. The idea of hospitality is central to the heart of the Gospel message, for God invites the lost into a place where they are named and known. When we practice hospitality, we embody this truth to the world.

This is affirmed again in 1 Timothy 5:10, where hospitality is listed as one of the primary virtues by which a woman can be known. More mysteriously, Paul suggests in Hebrews 13:2 that we never know who we might be sheltering when we open our homes. Paul also directly commands it in his lively list of exhortations to the Romans

(Romans 12:13). In Psalm 68:6, it says that God makes a home for the lonely, some versions read "He sets them in families." And, of course, there is the highly convicting passage in Matthew 25 where God says that the food and comfort we offer to the least of the people around us are offered directly to Him.

Start with Dinner

The most basic form of hospitality and the easiest to accomplish is simply to share a meal. Breaking bread with others brings people into immediate fellowship, and it is a theme mentioned often in Scripture. There is something truly beautiful about inviting guests into your home and giving them a sense of belonging at your dinner table. Be the bread breaker, be the life giver, and instill those beautiful qualities in your children. As part of this practice, include your children in all of the preparations. Here are some of the tasks I assigned my own kids:

Décor

This was the fun task, the one everyone loved. Depending on the season, I helped my children to select candles, placemats, seasonal decorations, and pretty dishes to create a lovely table for our guests. We also made sure every common room in the house had a candle or a little vase of flowers. They were so proud of the beauty they designed and loved to show it to our guests.

Setting the Table

"The world was my oyster but I used the wrong fork."
~ Oscar Wilde

Your children are never too young to learn how to set a lovely table ... correctly! Grab plastic placemats and draw a model for your children using a dry-erase marker. Then, let them practice putting the correct utensils and napkin in place. This will encourage your little ones and boost their confidence. When your children get a bit older and don't need the plastic mat example anymore, have them set the table for events and parties at home. This will encourage them to take pride in their part of the hospitality and, when done together, creates that teamwork that is always desirable between siblings.

Cultivating Beauty for Your Creative Types

Inspire creativity at the dinner table by encouraging your children to help out by lighting candles, creating homemade centerpieces, or going for a walk in the family garden to create a lovely floral arrangement. Let an artistic child make place cards with guests' names to be set at their seat at the table, or have them draw and decorate a menu to show guests.

Don't Forget the Food!

A huge element of hospitality at the dinner table is deciding on what delectable goodies you will prepare! Food is the great connector of people and one of the great, colorful delights of life. Give each child a special responsibility in this realm. One person can be in charge of getting the guests' drink orders while other children help out in the meal preparation. Perhaps you have a baking expert in your home! Allow one of your children to hone the fun, delicious responsibility of baking cookies as a sweet end to the evening. Make the creation of the meal an event in which to savor the variety of tastes God has made.

> ## KEEP CALM AND CARRY ON MOM TIP
> *Don't become discouraged if your children aren't always perfectly perky and excited to help with the hospitality dinner tasks. It takes time and dedication to form family habits. Try putting on your child's favorite music while they set the table and light the candles to add unique personality to the moment and keep them inspired. Remember: hospitality is joyous! It should be a fun, rewarding experience for the family to take part in as a team.*

Create Hospitable Habits

Before you even send the invitation, there are ways that you can be training your children in how to relate to guests. Our home always seemed to be a beautiful revolving door for guests. Whether it was a family holiday, a tea party, or a Bible study, my children knew that our home was inviting, welcoming, and ready to be filled. Teaching your children simple, basic etiquette will give them the confidence to be wonderful hosts alongside their mama.

Talk it Out Before You Walk it Out

As mothers, we have all been guilty at one point or another when we find ourselves expecting our children to understand concepts that we have *never* talked through with them before. Before you throw your next big soiree, chat with your children about some of the social skills, manners, and etiquette that you've ingrained as your family ways. Talk to your little ones, especially those who tend to be more introverted, about different possible outcomes. Allow them to visualize the circumstances and have an idea of how the night may go prior to overwhelming them with a packed house.

In our family before guests arrived (or before we *became* guests at someone else's house) we always played "thumbs up, thumbs down." This is how it went:

"Do we frown at guests and slam the door?" *Thumbs down!*

"Do we smile and take their coats and show them where to go?" *Thumbs up!*

"Do we rush ahead and take the first plate of food?" *Thumbs down!*

"Do we honor our guest and let them go first?" *Thumbs up!*

It greatly helped to set our children's expectations.

Preparation is Love

In our home, we love to write the names of our guests on a little chalkboard sign outside our front door. It is a way for us to make our guests feel welcomed before they even step foot in our home. Encourage your children to get creative and hands on in the set-up process! Just like adding candles to a table adds an extra touch of warmth, your children can go above and beyond when they are older by adding a slice of lemon to the water, making a beautiful welcome sign, creating homemade place cards for dinner, or designing fun labels for pitchers with your various beverages!

Once the Doorbell Rings

When all of the hard work and preparations are done, the door is being knocked upon, and the bell is ringing, the fun begins! Have your children greet guests by looking them in the eye, smiling, taking their coats, and offering them something to drink. Remember that different children can take on different responsibilities, and always think about their unique personalities and strengths prior to assigning tasks. But be sure to help your extroverts *and* your introverts understand the special duty they have as hosts to make their guests feel welcome.

For the Overnight Guests

We love to make others feel comfortable and at home if they will be spending the night. When we have overnight guests, we create a welcoming basket in their room with a bottle of water, fresh flowers, and some of our favorite chocolates. Your children will have a blast creating the welcome baskets for your friends or family. Be creative.

And Remember, Encourage Your Little Hosts!

Assign different jobs to different children. Always remember to encourage them and remind them that they are doing a great job! Affirm their effort and creativity. Children are no different than adults; if they feel unappreciated, unnecessary, or burnt out, they won't find joy in hospitality. Remember how crucial it is that your children find value and delight as they learn to serve others.

KEEP CALM AND CARRY ON MOM TIP

When you are ready to take a break and rest in the midst of preparing for a house full of guests, set your children up with a craft table to keep them entertained. Get out a few paintbrushes, a small can of chalkboard paint, and glasses of your choice that have a good amount of flat space (mason jars work quite well). Have your children create the party favors for your guests by painting a small square of

> *chalkboard paint onto each glass or jar. Then, allow your children to have fun coming up with a lovely place to display these homemade favors. Set out chalk and allow each guest to write their name on their glass so they don't get mixed up, and afterward, they can take their special, homemade goodie home with them to keep!*

The Key Elements of Being a Great Host

You may never know the impact you've had on someone's life simply by taking the time to allow him or her into the place you call home. When your children see the way your family values hospitality, not only will their lives be changed, they will also be changing the lives of others through the instruction you have given them. It is a ripple effect. Below, I have outlined a little acronym we found useful as we cultivated hospitality in our children.

Becoming a H.O.S.T.

H is for Home

Home is not only where the heart is. Home is where family dwells. Home is the special place where we allow God into every little nook and cranny of our lives. Because of this, it is also a gift we can give to others. Invite others into your home fearlessly, and allow your children to take part in the cultivating of true fellowship.

O is for Opened Hearts

We don't deserve any of what God has given us. The grace of family, the gift of home is not a "right" we can take for granted, or a possession we were meant to own in isolation and hoard away. God has entrusted each family to create a home that is a beautiful shelter. Part of our job is to teach our children how to open up their home, open up their hearts, and allow others to come into this very special place.

S is for Sacred

Not many people have a place of refuge, a beautiful oasis, or a safe haven. As a mother, you have the ability to turn your home into a sacred place where guests can become refueled, refreshed, and better equipped to take on the tasks that life may bring. Talk to your children about how important it is to make home a special, safe atmosphere in which God's love may be richly encountered.

T is for Trust

It is a blessing that we are not expected to reinvent the wheel. God isn't asking you to do crazy, unrealistic tasks in your home. The art of hospitality is within your reach, and it is within the reach of your children. Consistently read Scripture and study what God says about the home, and what He says about hospitality. Then, all you have to do is open up your heart and trust Him to love through you as you open the doors of your home.

WRAPPING UP THE GIFT:
PUTTING THE GIFT OF HOSPITALITY INTO MY CHILD'S LIFE

_____

_____

_____

_____

_____

_____

_____

_____

_____

_____

_____

_____

_____

_____

_____

_____

_____

_____

_____

_____

CHAPTER 9: INITIATIVE

The Gift of Taking Responsibility

"Therefore, to one who knows the right thing to do and does not do it, to him it is sin."

~ JAMES 4:17

"Success comes from taking the initiative and following up... persisting...eloquently expressing the depth of your love. What simple action could you take today to produce a new momentum toward success in your life?"

~ TONY ROBBINS

Storm clouds were forming in the autumn Texas sky as I stood by my car and wondered what in the world to do. Clay was out of town at a meeting and I was supposed to drive a trailer full of books to a conference where I would be speaking. Having never hitched a trailer to a car before, and having a sore back to boot, I wasn't even sure where to begin. Eleven-year-old Joel saw me eyeing the trailer hitch suspiciously and ambled over to where I stood in our garage.

"What's wrong, Mom?"

I told him my dilemma.

"Mama, I'm not Daddy, but he always told me to take care of you and the kids. I think if I read the instructions and call Daddy, I will be able to get it all hooked up just right. Don't you worry. I'll help!"

And so he did. For the next couple of hours, Joel labored with the trailer, calling his dad to get advice, and managing to hook it up perfectly. He then helped me to load all the books, arranging them neatly so they wouldn't shift during the drive. His diligence continued throughout the trip that followed, as did his confidence. I found that conference easy because he always helped me when I had to back the car, spotted for me when I had to park, and generally pitched in wherever he could. I could never have done it without him, and I couldn't have been more proud of my Joel.

But I also felt a deep sense of joy in watching my son because I knew that he was reflecting the ideals we had trained him in since birth. When he was just a little boy we began to build a sense of self-government into the very psyche of Joel's mind. "You are a strong boy, Joel. You will be able to do many things if you just put your mind and will into it. It is a glory for a man to become self-reliant and dependable. We know that you will be the kind of young man that people will be able to depend upon."

We spoke those words to him over and over again. We included him in our work, and encouraged him to be responsible all on his own. Day after day, we pushed him a little closer toward becoming a master of his own heart, a man who lived by initiative instead of passivity. We wanted him to have the gift of becoming a self-governed man, not waiting to be told what to do, but taking initiative to grow and give in every sphere of his life.

God has given us the great responsibility to subdue every aspect of the life he has entrusted to us. But far too often we sit on the sidelines of our own lives. The role of a spectator is easy to play and it is tempting to watch the world from a safe distance, observing the brokenness, possibility, and need, but simply waiting for someone else to stand up and do God's work. But do we want to be wallflowers in the dance of our own world, even our own lives? Do we want to raise our children to stand aside, or do we want them to stand up, answer God's call to live well, and dance their way through life?

When I was just out of college and a new staff member with Campus Crusade, I heard one of my directors give a powerful talk on the need for missionaries in then-Communist Poland. As he spoke, I felt conviction grow in my heart. Those people needed us to help them! When the talk was over and a general invitation was given to join the new team being formed to take the Gospel to Poland,

I rushed forward, sure I would be one of hundreds who wanted to apply. Instead, I found that I was one of only four.

Because of the great change that God's love had made in my own life, I was ready to do anything to bring that love to other people. God's love made me an initiator. But many people never listen to God's call in their hearts. As I began to raise my children, I remembered that call to Poland and the few who responded, and I resolved that I would help my children to be go-getters. I wanted them to be the ones who saw need and stepped forward to help. I wanted my kids to be active members of God's kingdom, and I knew that meant training them to take initiative in every area of their lives.

Two of the primary ways I did this was first, to encourage them in finding God's unique story for their lives, and second, teaching them to initiate rather than complain. Regarding the first, there is something truly powerful that comes to a child when they realize that God has a unique and specific purpose for their life. When people understand that they aren't just faceless workers to God, but rather are known and loved, they gain a sense of identity that comes from love. I talked often to my children about the story God was making around them, and the great deeds He wanted them to accomplish with their lives. I asked them what loves or passions God was forming in their hearts, and I helped them to pursue those. Writing for Sarah, music for Joel, acting for Nathan, and speech for Joy. As I called them to be initiators, to look for ways to help or give, I explained the significance of their responsibility. They were in training to take their place as heroes in God's kingdom story.

Clay and I often challenged our children with Scripture. We would read the following verses to our children and ask them questions:

Ephesians 2:10 – "For we are His workmanship, created in Christ Jesus for good works, which God prepared beforehand so that we would walk in them." *What good works do you think you should walk in? What do you think God has prepared for you to do?*

Colossians 1:10 – "[So] that you will walk in a manner worthy of the Lord, to please Him in all respects, bearing fruit in every good work and increasing in the knowledge of God." *What do you need to learn about God? What does it mean to bear fruit? Are you bearing fruit in your own life?*

2 Timothy 2:21 – "Therefore, if anyone cleanses himself ... he will be a vessel for honor, sanctified, useful to the Master, prepared for every good work." *What does it mean to be sanctified? Are you "prepared" to do any good work God asks of you?*

Another Scripture that we used came in handy when we dealt with attitudes of complaint or passivity. Galatians 6:5 is a convicting piece of Scripture. Read it in several different versions, as sometimes reading numerous versions of the Bible can greatly open your eyes to a brand new perspective. Consider how the words could apply to your life and the lives of your children today:

"For each one should carry their own load."

"For we are each responsible for our own conduct."

"For every person will carry his own luggage."

I found this highly convicting in my own life. These days, it is common to be passive. Many people will sit around and complain about why things aren't being done without ever learning to begin the work themselves.

Countless times in my life, I have waited and waited, hoping that a friend would magically call me and ask me to come over for dinner or that someone else would start a fellowship group for my kids. But as I encountered that verse in Galatians, I had to examine my own heart. Was I waiting around, expecting someone else to carry luggage that had my name on it?

One of the hardest and best things I have learned is how to look into a void that could be discouraging and create life around it instead. I quickly realized that if I was lonely, the easiest way to find friends was to be the initiator. When no one invited me to a group, I led my own. When nobody called to ask how my week was going, I decided to make a few phone calls of my own. And I passed this practice onto my children.

It's all too easy to get caught up in a cycle of throwing our own pity parties. That is a practice of which we are all naturally capable, especially children. We can sit around and mope, but it won't change a thing. One of the best gifts you can give your children is to be an initiator. Teach your children to be initiators of relationships and cultivators of friendships. Teach them to start a group where there is none. Teach them to encourage the lonely if no one else will, to feed the hungry, or start an outreach. If they want friends, tell them to ask someone over. If they want a job, encourage them to hone their skills, fill out an application, and dress well for the interview.

If your children can develop the skill of being an initiator, they will have the chance both to flourish in their own lives, but also to lead those who are waiting around for someone else to do the work. Raising children who are go-getters means continually challenging your children to optimism, hard work, and innovation. It was always my goal to love my children in a way that would give them the confidence to govern their own lives. This confidence inspires independence, and it gave my children the ability to think, dream, and set goals all on their own. Abraham Lincoln says this: "You cannot build character and courage by taking away a man's initiative and independence."

Courage and character begin with the energy of initiative. Together, they will equip your child to live with purpose, compassion, and independence.

Nurturing Initiation

Cultivate Ownership

Each of the following areas describes an arena in which you can help your child to have a sense of ownership for his or her own life. They need to feel that they are responsible for their words, actions, and choices.

Dare to Dream

Make a dream board with your children that will help them focus on goals and visualize what they are passionate about. Your dream board can be whatever kind of "board" that suits your home best and inspires your child the most (colorful poster board, cork board for various photos and magazine clippings, or chalkboard). Encourage your children to set individual goals, short term and long term, and to make their own plans for how they will achieve them. You could challenge your child to write a book, to finish a story, to raise money for a mission trip, or learn the guitar. Whatever it is, be sure that it kindles delight in your child and motivates ownership of their story. Whether you have a child who is more impacted by kinetic or visual learning, finding creative ways to ingrain these skills into their minds is a wonderful way for them to closely connect with what it truly means to be an initiator, goal setter, and go-getter!

Make Them Think

Learning to take the initiative, becoming a go-getter, and taking responsibility is a process that must be implemented into every part of your children's lives. Your children need these skills in order to conquer schoolwork, chores, creative endeavors, jobs, and so much more. One of the ways to encourage self-government and ownership in these areas is to make your children think. They need to be responsible for their own opinions, convictions, and integrity.

When your child asks you a question (whether regarding homework, friendship, curiosity, etc.), they are seeking your opinion and wise council. This is wonderful. But rather than simply giving them an answer, talk with them about different possible outcomes. Listen to their thoughts and encourage them to open up and share what ideas they might have to handle the particular situation. Discuss your convictions and help them to form their own. Independent action begins with independent thought.

Also, challenge them. If they are acting lazy or giving excuses for bad work, ask them if they really think what they have done is right. Challenge your children to be responsible for their actions by owning the attitudes beneath them (and paying the consequence for bad ones).

Adventures Make Leaders

When children have extremely structured lives and schedules with every detail penciled in, we are leaving them little room for practicing initiation, independence, and leadership. For them to be self-governed, there must be time for exploration. This is especially important in regard to boys. Allow them to make age appropriate, safe decisions on their own and have time to adventure in the backyard, in the home, and with their friends. Let them have hours in which to pretend, create, and explore.

Confession

As a mama of four children, I remember the many moments of sibling playtime when a crashing sound would come from the playroom followed by a very rare silence. When none of my children made a peep, it often meant that chaos had occurred. These situations could quickly turn into a lot of "he said, she said" filled with evasions from children who did not want to take the blame. The same could be said about many of the "fusses" I simply hated as a mom. It is crucial that we raise children who are able to take responsibility for their own actions by being open, honest, and willing to own their lives. No matter how long it took, I sat the kids down and talked with them until the truth was confessed and actions were owned.

Initiation in the Arts

Whether you are rehearsing for a musical, disciplining yourself to play an instrument, writing a story, or striving to learn a new move in ballet, being involved in the creative arts requires a lot of responsibility and dedication. Artistic endeavors are arenas of creativity and skill. Whether your child is naturally artistic or not, all children can benefit from the creative atmosphere of the arts. Let your children audition for a play (and pick a song and monologue all their own), sign them up for lessons in piano, guitar, or something more exotic (children's orchestras can be wonderful things). Give them lessons in photography, watercolor, or sketching. Whatever it is, give them the chance to soar creatively, to test their mental limits, and make something new.

Special Duties

Empower your children by giving them a specific area of work within the home for which they are directly responsible. A particular room, an area in the yard, the care of the dog, or the baking of cookies, whatever it is, give your children the chance to be the master of that area of work. Challenge them to bring their intelligence and creativity to their task, and help them to consider it as their gift to the family.

Telling the Truth

Talk to your children about why honesty is so important in the family. Self-governance begins with ownership of one's actions and words. Your children need to know that dishonesty and deceit are cowardly. Part of this means honesty even in the face of failure, something you can model as a mother. By showing your children grace even when it is difficult, you will encourage them to be honest about their mistakes and failures. But always teach them to tell the truth, to own what they have said and done.

Keep Calm and Carry On Mom Tip

Self-governed children aren't developed overnight. Fight the temptation to become discouraged, and don't give up on the days when your children make a mess, tell a fib, and don't wash their own dishes (even when you've told them a thousand times). Have patience and continue to work together with them on developing these vital life skills.

Train Them in Leadership

Leadership skills are vital to many aspects of life. Not every child may seem a natural born "leader," but every child was made to think, serve, and lead by initiation. Unless you teach and practice the vision and expectation of leadership skills, it will be easy for your children to simply follow others. Your goal as a mom is to create children of such vision and conviction that they are compelled to put those dreams into practice, leading others to the goodness they can envision. Regardless of personality type (I had two introverts, two extroverts) your children need you to encourage and train them in the confidence that will enable them to lead when appropriate.

Begin with Encouragement

Words that affirm are like a shot of secret strength into the souls of your children. When you encourage them in their efforts and affirm their initiative to create, to help, or to encourage someone else, you are helping them to love choosing what is right. Tell them what a wonderful job they have done, or how proud you are of their creativity, or how much you see them growing in faithfulness. Affirm every good thing and it will continue to grow.

Let Them Lead

Leadership muscles are developed by self-governing action. Allow your children to make decisions when appropriate. Perhaps one of your children has wanted to select the next film for family movie night, or maybe they can throw out a couple of ideas for what to do after church on Sunday as a family. Ask them what ministry project they might propose for the family, or let them choose the décor for their own room. When we allow our children to make simple decisions, they will be better equipped to take on the more difficult choices that life will bring.

Leaders are Readers

Children need both independence of thought and an inner picture of excellence if they are going to lead well. Great books provide both. Your children need exposure to the great thinkers of the world if they are going to have minds sharpened to grapple with the difficult dilemmas and decisions of their time. But they also need the vivid beauty of stories to stock their minds and hearts with images of heroes who inspire them to lead, to work, and to own their own stories. Reading is a Clarkson family obsession because we all believe that stories shape souls and words form convictions in the hearts of heroes.

WRAPPING UP THE GIFT:
PUTTING THE GIFT OF INITIATIVE INTO MY CHILD'S LIFE

_____

_____

_____

_____

_____

_____

_____

_____

_____

_____

_____

_____

_____

_____

_____

_____

_____

_____

_____

Chapter 10: Patience

The Gift of Spiritual Muscle

"I can do all things through Him [Christ] who strengthens me."
~ Philippians 4:13

"Nothing in the world is worth having or worth doing unless it means effort, pain, difficulty … I have never in my life envied a human being who led an easy life. I have envied a great many people who led difficult lives and led them well."
~ Teddy Roosevelt

"**M**om, I just don't know if I can make it."
No mother wants to hear those words over the phone from a child living several thousand miles away. I shifted in my chair and held the receiver closer to my ear as Joel told me more.

"There's just so much to be done – I'm almost to finals and I have to compose several new pieces of music by next week, and I'm working as many extra hours as I can, but I also have a lot going on in the house where I'm living and, Mom, I'm just exhausted. I'm getting sick and I'm worried about everything and well ... what should I do?"

I took a deep breath. I prayed under my breath. I knew that Joel was carrying more than he thought he could bear. Driven to finish his degree early, he was taking a full class load, teaching music once a week at a local school, working in the college office and trying to compose the crucial piece for his senior recital. I knew that he must be afraid of failure. I knew he must be anxious, I knew his heart was probably racing, his head aching with worry. But I also knew my son. I knew his capacity. I knew he had a choice and I believed in his strength of soul to make it.

"Joel," I said, "I'm so sorry. I can't even imagine how much you must have to do and I don't know how you are able to compose such beautiful music so quickly. You have been so faithful in the past few months and I am so, so proud of you."

I heard the quiet on the other end of the phone as his breath grew slower.

"But Joel," I said, "I really believe God put you there so that you can learn everything you need to know about music. I think he's filling your heart with beautiful things and making you strong as you shoulder all this work. I know how hard everything is right now, but I believe in you with all my heart. I think you can make it. Remember your Joshua verse?"

When Joel was thirteen and struggling with a lack of confidence, he had memorized God's words to Joshua (Joshua 1:9): "Remember that I have commanded you to be strong and brave, so don't be afraid. The Lord your God will be with you everywhere you go." I repeated those words to him over the phone.

"I think God is preparing you to be a hero, to bring beautiful music into this world, but nothing good or holy is ever easy. I believe you are strong in your heart, Joel; I think you can make it."

"Okay, Mom."

I could hear the acceptance in his voice, the deep, mental breath he took as he quieted his heart and accepted the challenge. We talked for a long time after that, working through different problems. I told him to rest, to nourish his tired body. He talked through a friendship problem with me, and by the end, his voice was calm. When we hung up, I knew he would be okay.

Four months later, I stood at Joel's senior recital concert and watched a pianist perform his original composition. Crowds of people flocked around him afterwards, congratulating him on his work, affirming his excellence in study, friendship, and life. Joel beamed—my tall, strong, gentle son—and I knew that he was standing on the victorious side of a great battle of soul. And he had won.

Joel had become an overcomer. This strength came after long years of Clay's and my training, after a lifetime of small choices and his own soul-deep decision to press on. Joel's choice to overcome that year was one more step toward the work and life he is living now. It is one of my greatest honors as a mama to look at my Joel and know that he is a man God can use to accomplish great things in the kingdom because he chose to respond, to strengthen the muscles of his heart, and to endure.

One of the most vital things I have taught my children is how to fight the good fight. I knew that no matter how much love and goodness I gave to them, they would still have to live out their story in a fallen world. If they were going to flourish, I needed to teach them to be faithful in the midst of hard work and delayed success. They needed to learn how to wait, how to hope, and how to endure with grace.

We live in broken world and a hurry-up world, both of which mitigate against the building of soul strength into the heart of your child. As a parent, it is easy to focus so intensely on giving your child what is good in life that you forget to prepare them to meet sin, disappointment, suffering, delay. When children who have never encountered struggle confront the brokenness of life and the sinfulness of people, they are often in danger of a total crisis of faith.

But they are also in danger of impatience, of abandoning the hard work of becoming godly or working toward a great dream because they have believed the get-it-now messages of our culture. We are a fast-food, freeway, and entertainment society. The cultural messages your children hear every day in media, in stores, in movies and music, is that the most important thing is that they be happy. We live in a society that believes self-fulfillment is the ultimate goal, and then offers us a dozen things to buy or a quick fix to get us what we want.

But the road to godliness is a long one, and your children need to know that. Your children need to know that God works through seasons. That learning to wait is a large part of holiness, or creativity, or success of any kind. Teaching your child how to endure and how to wait with grace could change the whole story of their lives. This is a fallen world, and your children are guaranteed to meet pain, loneliness, and discouragement as they make their way within it, doubly so if they are pursuing holiness.

But just as a great athlete is trained by hours of hard work, by the discipline of his spirit, by hope in an outcome of excellence, you can train the souls and spirits of your children to endure in the face of hardship. You can teach them to walk in faith, to fight their battles well, and to become heroes in the story of God. I have known many years of loneliness, hard work, and sheer frustration with my children. We have talked for countless hours about what it means to endure, to live by faith, to walk with God in the midst of difficulty. As I have companioned my children through their hard times, I found that there was somewhat of a process, certain mindsets that helped me to give them what they needed and help them to choose to endure.

The first was simply sympathy. Our hearts were made for love, friendship, and joy, and when those things are absent, the natural human response is grief. I realized that one of the first things my children needed in order to endure was the knowledge that both God and I understood their struggle and shared in their frustration. No amount of simply gritting their teeth could get them through times of intense loneliness or burdensome work. The foundation of their strength needed to be their knowledge of God's compassion, and His promises to never leave them and to turn all things to their good.

Sarah has told me several times how much one thing I said meant to her. When she was in a time of intense loneliness, doubting God's love for her, I simply told her that I would have faith for her while she struggled and that my love and compassion were a picture of God's. I held her as she cried and that gave her the courage she needed to stand back up and keep on walking in faith. Heroes need advocates behind them, and that is one of the greatest roles that you can play as a mom.

But the second part of the process was to affirm my belief in my children's potential to be heroic. I needed to articulate for them, again and again, the reality that they could choose to be overcomers. In the midst of suffering, a person can take on one of two identities: the victim or the hero. Victims allow themselves to be identified and limited by their suffering. A hero overcomes it. I knew that my children needed me to articulate my belief that they could choose to be strong, to choose hope, to strengthen their heart muscles, and take their place in the battle for beauty, truth, and goodness. They needed me to help narrate a great story for them. As we walked together through hard times, I watched them begin to live the identity of someone who could work hard, endure, and overcome hardship.

Part of this, then, was training. My children needed to own their choices of godliness. I could sympathize and affirm, but eventually my children needed to make a choice to be strong all on their own. Strength of soul requires constant practice just like strength of muscle. If my children practiced self-pity, whining, and a woe-is-me attitude, I knew that they would become weak. So I confronted my children when their sadness became plain whining. I worked to help them change attitudes of self-pity to a focus on God's goodness. I pointed them to Scripture. I challenged them to choose, like David or Joseph, like Esther or Mary, to be heroic, because in the end, their story was in their own hands and they would answer to God for their choices.

Finally, I helped my children learn how to bring light to the darkness. In my own times of struggle, I have learned that one of the best ways to fight despair is to create life. We love a God who spoke light into darkness, who looked at what was formless and void and filled it with color and creation. In His image, we are called to the same creativity. So when Sarah was deeply lonely, I began a weekly tea date with her in which we had a lovely, sit-down tea all by ourselves. We became best friends. When we moved to a new place and had difficulty in finding friends, the kids and I hopped in the car and went for adventure days downtown and began to invite new friends to dinner. When Joel was unsure of his ability in music, I told him to listen to great composers, to practice every day, and he wrote the piece that gained him entrance to the school of his dreams.

Those who learn to endure, to wait, to work, have a unique power. They have the secret inner strength common to all heroes. Your children will bear the gift of patient endurance with them wherever they go, and it will help them to never give up.

Hero Training

Forming Heroic Hearts

The hardest part of becoming a hero is forming the attitudes of the heart. Whining, complaining, discouragement, defeatism; these, as I told my children, are *natural* responses to difficulty. A *supernatural* response is one based on a view of the world that says, "I can do all things through Christ who strengthens me." This requires the habit of faith, one you can build in your children by your own words and example.

Know and Memorize Scripture.

The basis for a holy and excellent life has to be faith in a holy and good God. Your children need to have Scripture in their minds so that when they meet discouragement and fear, they can speak words like this into their struggle:

- *I can do all things through Him [Christ] who strengthens me.* Philippians 4:13
- *Therefore, since we are surrounded by such a great cloud of witnesses, let us throw off everything that hinders and the sin that so easily entangles, and let us run with perseverance the race marked out for us. Let us fix our eyes on Jesus, the author and perfecter of our faith.* Hebrews 12:1
- *And without faith, it is impossible to please Him, for he who comes to God must believe that He is, and that He is a rewarder of those who seek Him.* Hebrews 11:6
- *For God has not given us a spirit of timidity, but of power, and of love, and discipline.* 2 Timothy 1:7

- No temptation has overtaken you but such as is common to man, and God is faithful, who will not allow you to be tempted beyond what you are able, but with the temptation will provide the way of escape also, so that you will be able to endure it. 1 Corinthians 10:13
- For who is God but the LORD, and who is a rock except our God, the God who girds me with strength and makes my way blameless, He makes my feet like hinds feet and sets me upon my high places. Psalm 18:31-32

Articulate Heroism

Encouragement is one of the great forces you can use to help your children become heroes. We can use our words to narrate life into a situation. Instead of berating your discouraged child, or verbalizing your disappointment, make a goal to constantly articulate your belief in them. "I know you can be a hero if you choose. I believe you can do this. I can't wait to see what God does with your life. I'm so proud of you. Keep trying. You're getting to be so strong. Don't give up." Let your words of affirmation be one of the primary voices in the lives of your children.

Hero Tales

One of the best and most delightful ways that you can teach your children what heroism looks like is by filling their imaginations with great stories. Read your children stories of biblical heroes, of missionaries, of people who lived their whole lives in love of God. We loved *Hero Tales* by Dave and Neta Jackson. Read your children stories of great historical figures like William Wilberorce, or Abraham Lincoln, who led whole countries in heroic ways. Read your children the stories of great scientists and artists who persevered in order to discover or create great things within their lifetimes. Every story you give your child helps them to have another picture of what it looks like to be brave, to be gracious, to endure hardship, and to win the race.

Forming Heroic Habits

Young Children

Challenge your children. Heroes need challenges. Children need a goal to work toward, a task to complete, an honor to attain in order to teach them endurance and fortitude. Before they even reach the point when they will confront real difficulty in life, give your children the chance to practice fortitude by letting them take on projects, goals, or dreams that require a lot of them. Consider the following:

Creative or Educational Projects

Children need to own their own dreams and goals. As your children grow old enough to have specific interests, challenge them to a project. A science project, the composition of a piece of music or the writing of a story, an outreach to neighborhood kids, a lemonade stand ... whatever interests your child. Help your children to own their ideas, to work for their creation, and to see their projects to fulfillment.

Long-Term Goals

When our kids were just learning to read, we made some kind of a chart for each of them (e.g., for Sarah, we drew a picture of a house on a poster board, with a hundred little windows) on which they could mark the number of books they had read. When they reached our set goal of one hundred, they earned some sort of prize that would thrill them. For Joel, a day at the local theme park, for Nathan, a trip to a magician's conference (where he could learn sleight-of-hand), for Sarah and Joy, an overnight with Mom at a local hotel or B&B. The goal sometimes took months to complete, but the prize was worth the wait and effort. As they got older, it might be saving for a new bike, working with us at the office to earn money for a vacation, or raising money for a mission trip.

KEEP CALM AND CARRY ON MOM TIP

When life is hard, sometimes the best thing you can do is to make a cup of hot chocolate and do something fun. This is a form of building courage in and of itself. Give yourself and your children grace in the midst of struggle.

Older Children

When your children reach that age when they are beginning to come up against struggle, disappointment, or the need for great faithfulness, you have the chance to disciple and encourage them in a special way. You can be like Christ, walking with them through the darkness, teaching them how to bring light. These are some of the ways we walked with our kids in times of discouragement:

Disciple

Just as Jesus sometimes took a few of the disciples away alone, when our kids were beginning to mature spiritually and grapple with deep issues, we made sure to take them away for special time with Mom or Dad. Sometimes it was just a coffee date, sometimes an overnight as part of a ministry trip, sometimes just a backrub at night, but these times were designed to give us the chance to talk, *a lot*. We wanted to really hear and understand what was going on in the souls of our kids.

As part of this, we began to disciple our kids intensely and individually. As parents, we knew we often presented God to our children as they were just beginning to know Him. We wanted them to have Scripture in their hearts and wisdom in their heads as they set out.

Celebrate

No matter how much I wanted to as a mom, I couldn't conjure up friends for my kids when they were lonely or make their way easy when life was hard. But I could equip them to make it through with grace and even enjoyment. I made sure to teach my kids how to celebrate. Wallowing wasn't a Clarkson option. If my kids were down and discouraged, I listened, I hugged, I talked, and then I set them to doing something lovely. Have a cup of tea. Watch a movie. Go to an art museum. Listen to music. Light a candle. Read a book. I consistently helped my children to create life around themselves, even in the midst of discouraging days, and I entered into the fun with them.

Some of my favorite memories are from the days when we decided to cook an autumn feast and invite all the neighbors. Or bake three-dozen cookies and deliver them to new friends. Or the day we hopped in the car with a picnic and visited a string of Amish farms in the Tennessee hills. Or the day we found a tiny tea room in a nearby downtown. All of the above events came about because of discouragement that was turned into an opportunity for celebration. God spoke light into the darkness. So did we.

Challenge

Nothing strengthens your children for spiritual challenge like a challenge of another kind. Give your children, especially when they are at the age to need an independent identity, the chance to take on a big challenge. We believed in empowering our children to begin to pursue (or discover through experimentation) their vocations while they were still in high school. Sarah wanted to be a writer, so we challenged her to complete, edit, and publish a whole book. Joel wanted to be a musician, so he wrote, recorded, and sold his own album of original music. Nate wanted to be an actor, so we let him pursue admission to an acting school in New York City. Joy wanted to be a communicator, so we let her join a speech and debate team even as she began classes at a local community college.

All of these endeavors began when our kids were trying to figure out life and their part within it. Often, they completed these challenges in the midst of real spiritual struggle, loneliness, or confusion. But the presence of a creative challenge focused their hearts, helped them to learn focus of mind and discipline of emotion, and gave them something to be proud of at the end. In the midst of turmoil, they established an identity as overcomers, as creators, as adults.

WRAPPING UP THE GIFT:
PUTTING THE GIFT OF PATIENCE INTO MY CHILD'S LIFE

_____

_____

_____

_____

_____

_____

_____

_____

_____

_____

_____

_____

_____

_____

_____

_____

_____

_____

_____

_____

_____

_____

_____

_____

_____

_____

WRAPPING UP THE GIFT:
PUTTING THE GIFT OF PATIENCE INTO MY CHILD'S LIFE

_____

_____

_____

_____

_____

_____

_____

_____

_____

_____

_____

_____

_____

_____

_____

_____

_____

_____

_____

BONUS CHAPTER: READING

The Gift of a Story-formed Life
By Sarah Clarkson

"And do not be conformed to this world, but be transformed by the renewing of your mind ..."

~ ROMANS 12:2

"How many a man has dated a new era in his life from the reading of a book."

~ HENRY DAVID THOREAU

Six years ago, I sent a copy of *Anne of Green Gables* to a little girl I have never met and probably never will. All I knew about her was that she was eleven years old and that she'd never heard of my favorite childhood literary heroine, Anne. I met her mother on a flight to Canada as we discussed the merits of Prince Edward Island, the tiny island in the Maritimes where Lucy Maud Montgomery set the story that companioned generations of young girls through their childhood and adolescence. The mother, in all her trips to that island, had never heard of Anne. When she told me of her daughter, I simply couldn't bear the thought of a little girl growing up without the world offered in the *Anne* books. I got her address and shipped a copy off as soon as I got home.

I tell this story in my guide to children's literature, *Read for the Heart,* because that encounter was one of the kindling causes behind the writing of that book. For days after that airplane conversation, I was troubled. At first, I couldn't quite understand why. After all, I told myself, *Anne of Green Gables* is just one story. Beautiful as it is, could it really change a little girl's life? But as I got home and began to go back through the favorite stories of my childhood, mulling the idea of writing a guide to children's books, I realized the cause behind my troubled soul. As I delved back into the story-worlds that companioned my girlhood, encountered the characters that were the heroes and heroines looming large in my imagination, I realized how deeply the books I read had shaped my vision of life. My own ideas of courage, of creativity, of friendship, of beauty, were greatly formed by the stories that filled my mind and heart in my earliest years.

The distress I felt for the flight attendant's daughter came from my realization that Anne's world created a world within my heart that influences the way I live today. It's a world I think every girl needs. The community pictured in the Anne books, the way Anne encounters creation as a living thing, the "kindred" friendships she sees as treasures, her lively imagination ... each of these influenced the way I live, relate, and envision my own life as an adult. Her story formed my own. When I mentioned this to several writer friends currently at work on children's books of their own, they immediately agreed. The *Anne* books formed the sensibilities of generations of girls, affirming family, beauty, community, and imagination. But, as one friend pointed out, her story has begun to fade from the literary scene of late. The stories forming the hopes and expectations of girls today tend toward those portraying teenage romance, vampire adventures, or the supernatural.

"What different worlds girls today have in their souls," said my friend.

Her observation is key, and it drives one of the reasons I am passionate about speaking to parents on the vital importance of giving the gift of great stories to their kids. We are all story-formed souls. We live within the story of our own lives and are shaped by the stories of others, and by the stories we *read*. Each story that a child encounters in their earliest years, each image conjured by their imagination, each character encountered, each landscape imagined shapes the person that child will become.

First, stories form a child's expectation of the world. What is required of a good person? What does it mean to be good? What does it mean to be heroic? What is beautiful? What actions are good, and what do those look like? What is evil? What are the consequences of certain choices?

Every story a child reads provides the answers to these fundamental questions about the nature and goal of life. There is no such thing as a neutral story. Stories always communicate, and they speak in the powerful language of image. In a story, abstract ideas like good and evil are enfleshed in the actions of characters, the beauty of landscapes, the choices and consequences of each person in the story. Great stories communicate a certain idea of what it means to be human and what ought to be desired and fought for in the world. Thus, it matters immensely that children read great books because every story that they encounter helps them to answer those fundamental questions concerning who they will be and what they ought to become.

Stories are your ally as a parent in forming your children to have a moral imagination. Stories help children to envision goodness, and they also make it desirable by clothing it in foreign lands and times, and in characters of humor, fire, and depth. Stories help children to "taste and see" what it means to live to the fullest and with integrity.

But the second thing that stories do is that they help your child to form an interior world. This has implications both spiritually and educationally. We live in a world of such activity, such constant outward expression, and such all-immersing technology that it is easy to forget the life of the mind, the inner world of the soul. Children especially are increasingly caught up in the distraction of technology, and in the cultural push toward minute-by-minute entertainment. This has consequences on several levels.

First, on an educational level, numerous studies have shown how necessary reading is to educational success. Media technology distracts the mind, while reading develops the brain. Some studies suggest that reading is the golden key in helping children to succeed, the first skill they need in order to grasp the ideas and concepts they encounter in every other subject.

But on a more spiritual level, when children live hurried, distracted, or technology-driven lives, the imagination gets entirely neglected. The human imagination is a powerful force, one that parents must cultivate in their children if they want to nurture creativity, independence of thought, and even spiritual sensitivity. The imagination is an interior realm where creativity begins, where ideas are conceived, where children encounter the mystery of realities that exist beyond the confines of what they merely see.

Great books enter into the process of cultivating imagination because they *are* works of imagination. When you give your child a good story to read, you are giving them the opportunity to exercise the muscles of their brain by enfleshing the words they are reading into pictures within their minds. Stories give children space in which to think, quiet in which to go deeply within their own thought. Educationally, this provides the brain the chance to encounter new language, to sift through new ideas, to add new concepts to its store of knowledge. Spiritually, stories help your children to create a rich interior world, an imagination stocked with the imagery and color of your child's own inner creation. Stories create space in a hurry-up world in which a child can wonder, imagine, and eventually create.

"Today a reader, tomorrow a leader," (Margaret Fuller) is a quote passed around in many forms, but one that will continue to be repeated because of its truth. The act of reading and the cultivation of imagination will equip your child with the vocabulary, the vision, and the inner world necessary for them to think and lead independently within their own world. Great stories will shape the great story you want your children to live.

My own parents grasped this early on. I count it one of the greatest gifts of my life that I was raised in a home crammed with books. The fact that my mom required me to read every single afternoon began a lifelong habit of reading in me that I cannot escape to this day. My parents were careful to choose books of literary and spiritual excellence, and they gave me free reign throughout my childhood in exploring the treasure on offer in our library.

As an adult now, I can honestly and very passionately say that the stories I read as a child shaped my spirit to a taste for courage and innovation. Stories have companioned me through times of struggle, giving me a vision to work toward. And they have shown me what it is possible for me to become. There are few greater gifts you can offer your child than the gift of a reading life. I am eternally grateful to my parents for a childhood crammed with good books. Yours will be too; I guarantee it.

Kick Start the Story-formed Life

Half-Hour a Day

Habits are the hardest things to begin, and the easiest to carry out once they are well founded. Help your children to form a lifelong habit of reading by encouraging them to read at least half an hour a day. Picture books, historical fiction, classics, poetry, mystery, biography, whatever tickles their fancy at first, help them to begin that habit of reading each day. When they are older, up the challenge to an hour.

Read Aloud

Not all children will be natural readers. And even for those who are, the gift of daily read-aloud times with a parent provides a companionship in the reading lifestyle that makes it a joyful practice. Create a culture of reading in your home by making this a daily, family rhythm.

Audiobooks

Do you spend any time in the car? Are you going on a road trip? Put away the DVDs and electronic games and get everyone together in listening to an audiobook. Choose intriguing stories or humorous ones, tales that will get the whole family eager for another jaunt in the car. Some of our family favorites were *Cheaper by the Dozen*, *The Treasure-Seekers*, and the dramatized *Chronicles of Narnia* produced by Focus on the Family.

Library Excursions

Make a trip to the library a family event. Take your kids to the children's section and let them choose several books of their own to check out (in addition, of course, to those you choose for them as well!). Make it a treasure hunt, an expedition into the land of imagination. You never know what you'll find!

Books as Decoration

I have always loved the Anna Quindlen quote that goes, "I would be most content if my children grew up to be the kind of people who think decorating consists mostly in building enough bookshelves." Indeed. One of the best ways that you can cultivate the reading life in your home is simply to have books all around. This doesn't mean decorating only with bookshelves, but it does mean picture books in baskets, shelves of children's classics, coffee tables with a few picture books or art tomes open, and at least a tiny library if at all possible. Make books accessible, present, and inviting.

Used Books

The process of outfitting your home with books doesn't have to be an expensive one. Go for bookish treasure hunts at garage sales, on eBay, at library sales (great resource!), and in your local used-books stores. There are countless cheap ways that you can build an excellent home library.

Reading Dates

Some of my favorite memories from childhood are from the times my mom took me out to a café, or set up a mom and me only time in our home in order to read aloud favorites like *Little Women, The Girl of the Limberlost,* or *Little House on the Prairie.* The delight of savoring a story with my mom remains in my heart to this day.

WRAPPING UP THE GIFT:
PUTTING THE GIFT OF READING INTO MY CHILD'S LIFE

_____

_____

_____

_____

_____

_____

_____

_____

_____

_____

_____

_____

_____

_____

_____

_____

_____

_____

_____

_____

_____

THANK YOU!

We so appreciate your purchase of *The 10 Gifts of Wisdom*. If you have enjoyed what you found here, we invite you to visit Sally at her blog where she writes regularly on motherhood, discipleship, and faith.

You can find her at: **www.itakejoy.com**

If you enjoyed this book, you may also enjoy the following titles on motherhood and parenting from Sally and others (all available through www.wholeheart.org):

The Mission of Motherhood by Sally Clarkson

This is Sally's exploration of the "big picture" biblical design of God for motherhood, a vision that transcends cultures and current trends. Drawing on challenging insights from Scripture and her own experience as a mom, Sally paints a biblical and very personal portrait of motherhood that reveals the heart of God for all mothers of all times.

The Ministry of Motherhood by Sally Clarkson

In a personal and devotional style, Sally addresses how a mother can spiritually shape and influence the precious lives entrusted to her care by looking to the life and ministry of Jesus as he trained his disciples.

Desperate by Sally Clarkson and Sarah Mae

Follow the mom-to-mom, heart-to-heart conversations of Sarah Mae, a young mom in the trenches with three children, and Sally, a seasoned mentor mom, as they discuss the eternal value of motherhood, the difficulties of living it well, and the grace to be found in the midst of the journey.

Our 24 Family Ways: A Devotional Guide by Clay Clarkson

Clay's "just add Bible" family devotional and discipleship resource based on 24 statements of biblical family values. Complete with daily devotionals and pictures for your children to color.

Read for the Heart: Whole Books for Wholehearted Families by Sarah Clarkson

With over a thousand recommendations and reviews, insightful essays, and personal stories, Sarah provides a guide for parents who want to navigate the wonderful world of children's literature.

Heartfelt Discipline by Clay Clarkson

Clay's insights into what Scripture really says about childhood discipline, the path of life, and the heart of your child.

Educating the WholeHearted Child by Clay Clarkson

Clay's exploration and explanation of WholeHearted Learning, a discipleship and literature based model of Christian homeschooling.

The Mom Walk by Sally Clarkson

Personal stories and biblical insights after 20 years of parenting on what it means to walk with God as a mother on the path you have been given.

Seasons of a Mother's Heart by Sally Clarkson

Sally's first book, written with homeschool mothers in mind, filled with stories, biblical insights, and personal reflections from the various seasons of motherhood.